NCERT Practice

WorkBook

Mathematics
Math-Magic

Class

2

arihant

Arihant Prakashan (School Division Series)

✳arihant

Arihant Prakashan (School Division Series)

All Rights Reserved

ॐ **Administrative & Production Offices**

Regd. Office

'Ramchhaya' 4577/15, Agarwal Road, Darya Ganj, New Delhi -110002
Tele: 011- 47630600, 43518550

ॐ **Head Office**

Kalindi, TP Nagar, Meerut (UP) - 250002
Tel: 0121-7156203, 7156204

ॐ **Sales & Support Offices**

Agra, Ahmedabad, Bengaluru, Bareilly, Chennai, Delhi, Guwahati, Hyderabad, Jaipur, Jhansi, Kolkata, Lucknow, Nagpur & Pune.

PO No : TXT-XX-XXXXXXX-X-XX

Published by Arihant Publications (India) Ltd.

For further information about the books published by Arihant, log on to www.arihantbooks.com or e-mail at info@arihantbooks.com

Follow us on   

PRODUCTION TEAM

Publishing Managers
Keshav Mohan, Amit Verma

Project Head
Ashwani

Project Editor
Amit Tanwar

Cover Designer
Bilal Hashmi

Inner Designer
Ankit Saini

Proof Readers
Akash Sharma

Workbook, Why?

"Knowledge will not be with you for Long Unless You Practice"

This quotation answer the above question 'Workbook, Why?' perfectly, i.e. Workbooks are made to give the students practice required to achieve perfection & mastery in the subject. These are the only Workbooks, which are strictly based on **NCERT, the only recommended books by Govt. of India & CBSE** (reference Circular No. Acad-41/2015 dated 20th July, 2015).

Given below is the detailed description of Workbook and some of its special features

ONLY WORKBOOK BASED ON NCERT

NCERT textbooks are the only textbooks, which have been prepared according to National Curriculum Framework, which discourages the idea of rote learning rather they focus on understanding and try to make the students able to identify the way of problem solving.

Keeping the importance of NCERT textbooks in mind we have prepared this Workbook, strictly based on NCERT content, this Workbook will complement NCERT by providing practice on the material given in each chapter of NCERT textbook, making the students understand the chapter completely.

WORKBOOK- PURPOSE, USE & FEATURES

This Workbook, through its **numerous exercises** having different **variety of questions** covering each and every fact of NCERT, will prove to be **equally useful** for both, **Classroom** and at **Home.** One more purpose of this Workbook is to provide the students a **systematic practice** of the content taught in the class and what they study in the textbooks.

Some special features of this workbook are

- Complete Coverage of each chapter for complete practice
- Different variety of questions; Fill in the Blanks, True-False, Matching, Multiple Choice Questions, Word Problems, etc.
- Many Questions given in each chapter are related with day-to-day activities making them interesting to solve.
- Keeps the students actively engaged with the content and develop enquiry skills.

WORKBOOK-DESIGNED TO IMPROVE SUBJECT ABILITIES

All the material given in this workbook is tailored to suit subject content with equal support on learning, which will surely help students to boost their abilities and confidence in the subject.

We look forward for the feedback from students, teachers and parents for the further improvement of the contents of this book. We will try to update the contents according to your feedback in further editions of this Workbook.

The Publisher

Contents

What is Long, What is Round?

1 Identify and write each object given below as long or round.

(i) 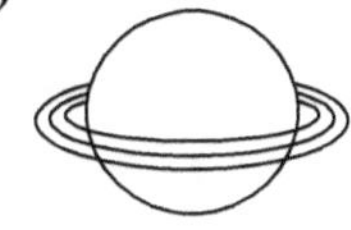 __________

(ii)  __________

(iii) 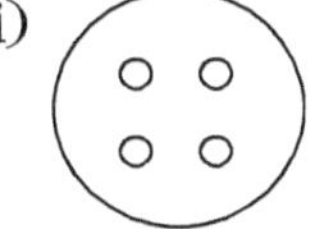 __________

(iv) 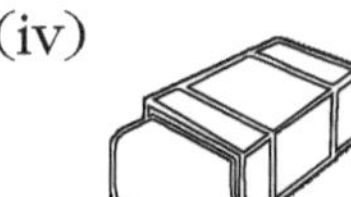 __________

(v)  __________

(vi)  __________

(vii) 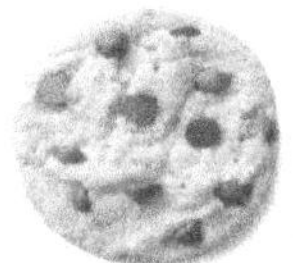 __________

(viii) 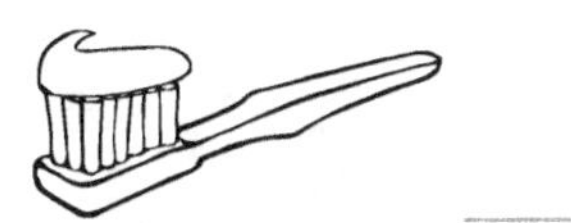 __________

2 Identify and write each object that can roll and can slide.

(i) ___________

(ii) ___________

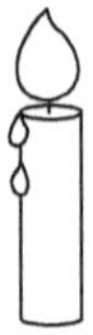

(iii) ___________

(iv) ___________

(v) ___________

(vi) ___________

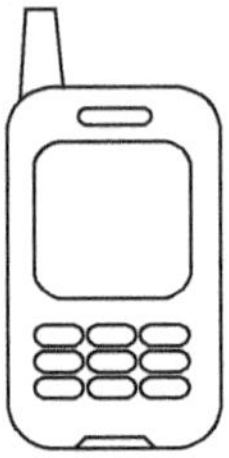

(vii) ___________

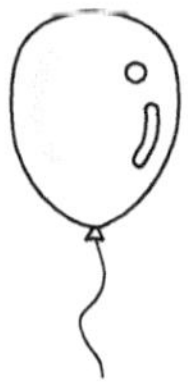

(viii) ___________

(ix) ___________

(x) ___________

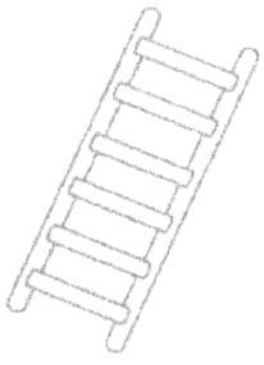

(xi) ___________

(xii) ___________

3 Draw or paste the things in the table given below. One has been done for you.

	Things which roll	**Things which slide**	**Things which both roll and slide**
(i)			
(ii)			
(iii)			
(iv)			

4 Look around you and draw any two objects that are long in the given space.

Example:

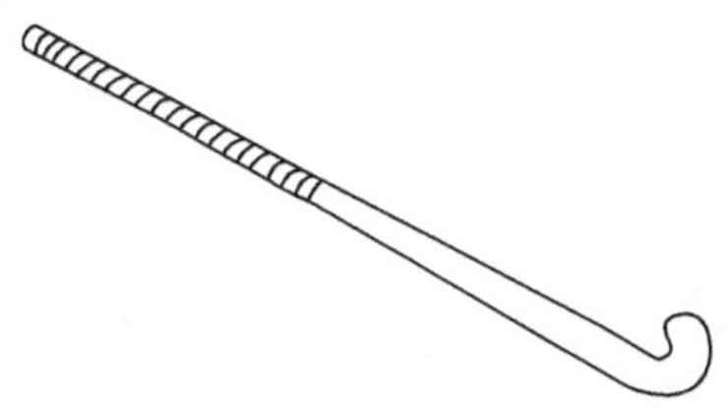

5 Which of the following objects have only two flat surfaces? Tick (✓) them.

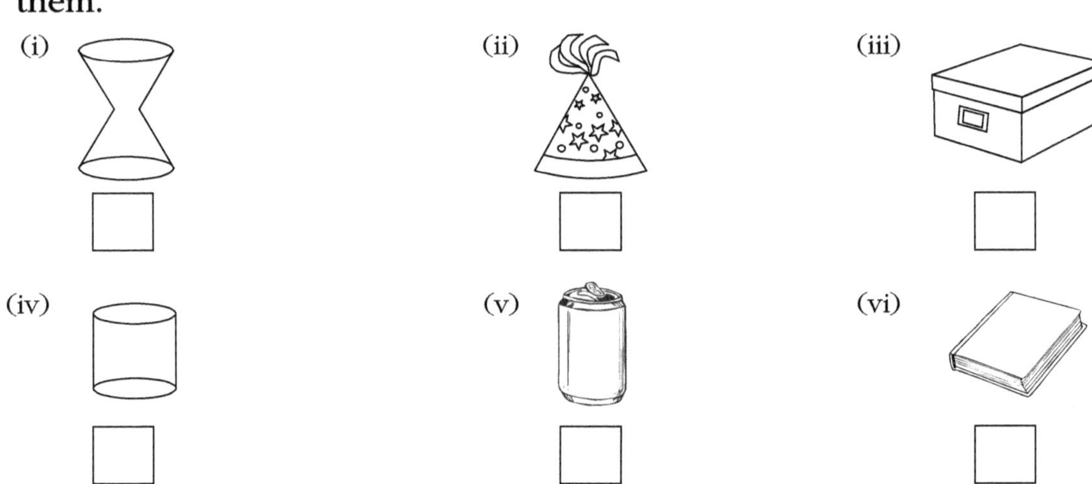

6 Circle the objects given below which can be used to form a tower by putting same object over one another.

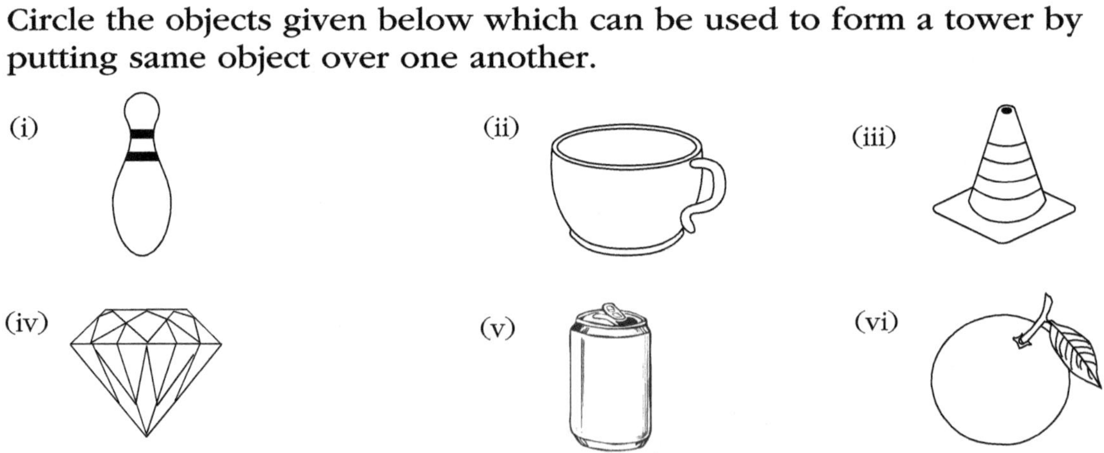

7 **Fill in the blanks.**

(i) A glue stick is —————— and its bottom is ——————. (long, round)

(ii) A cone has one —————— and has —————— bottom surface. (corner, flat)

(iii) An orange can —————— and a chocolate can ——————. (slide, roll)

(iv) A hockey stick can —————— and a hockey ball can ——————. (roll, slide)

8 **Match the following objects with their shapes.**

(i) 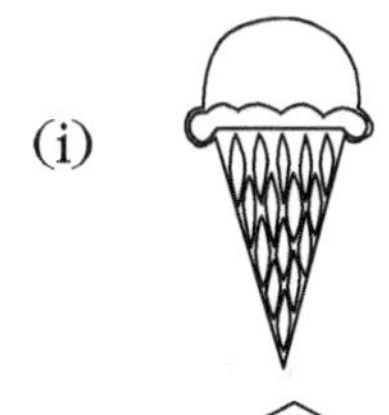

(a) 

(ii) 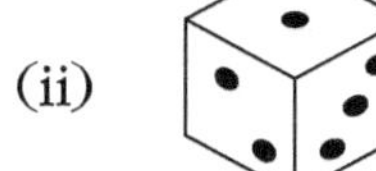

(b) 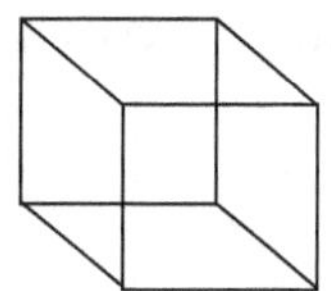

(iii) 

(c) 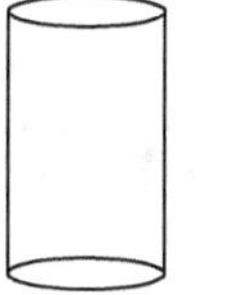

(iv) 

(d) 

9 **Tick (✓) the name of the given shapes.**

(i) 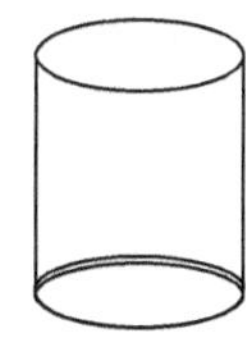
(Cone/Cube)
  (a)   (b)

(ii)
(Cube/Cone)
  (a)   (b)

(iii)
(Cylinder/
(a)
Cuboid)
(b)

(iv)
(Cylinder/
(a)
Cuboid)
(b)

Chapter 2

Counting in Groups

1 Fill in the blanks with the correct number of objects.

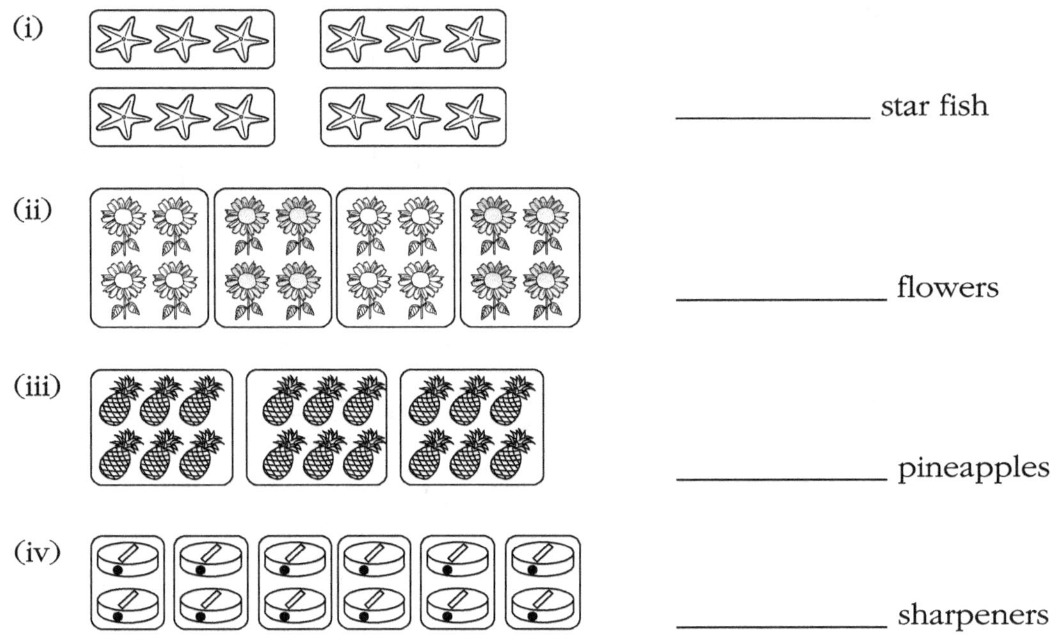

(i) _____________ star fish

(ii) _____________ flowers

(iii) _____________ pineapples

(iv) _____________ sharpeners

2 Without actual counting, find the total number of objects and fill in the blank space. One has been done for you.

(i)

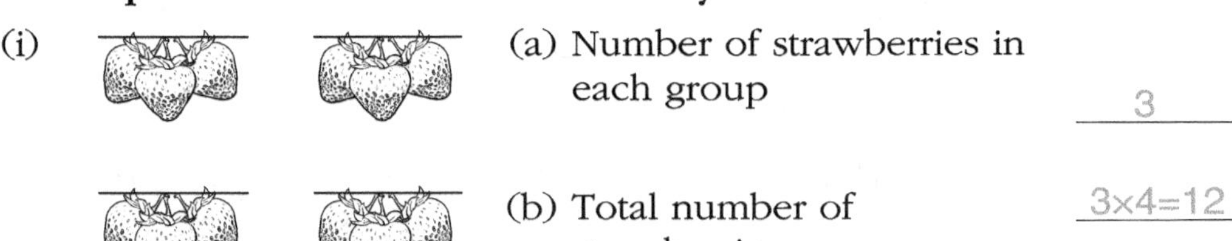

(a) Number of strawberries in each group   _____3_____

(b) Total number of strawberries   __3×4=12__

(ii) 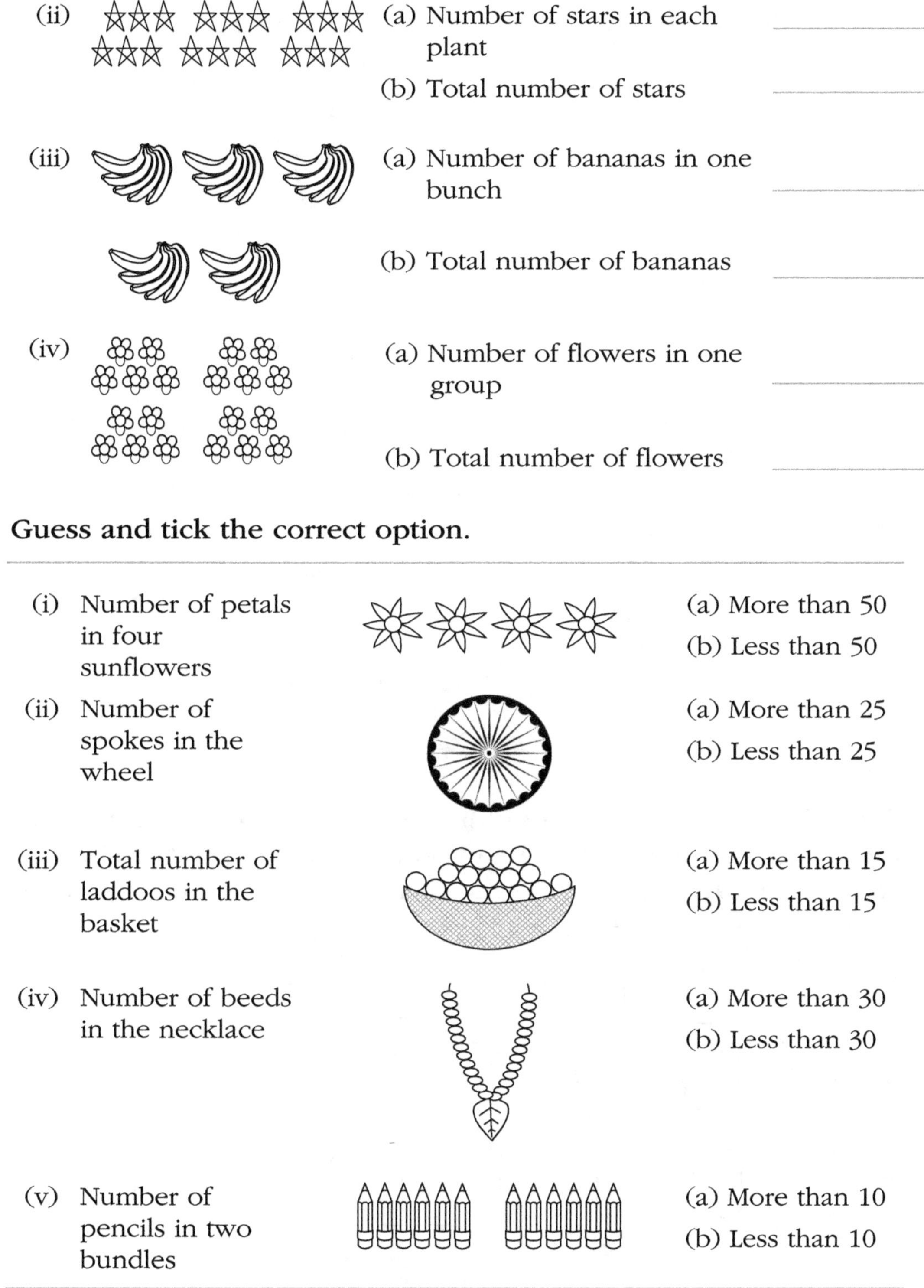

    (a) Number of stars in each plant   _______

    (b) Total number of stars   _______

(iii)

    (a) Number of bananas in one bunch   _______

    (b) Total number of bananas   _______

(iv)

    (a) Number of flowers in one group   _______

    (b) Total number of flowers   _______

3 Guess and tick the correct option.

(i) Number of petals in four sunflowers
  (a) More than 50
  (b) Less than 50

(ii) Number of spokes in the wheel
  (a) More than 25
  (b) Less than 25

(iii) Total number of laddoos in the basket
  (a) More than 15
  (b) Less than 15

(iv) Number of beeds in the necklace
  (a) More than 30
  (b) Less than 30

(v) Number of pencils in two bundles
  (a) More than 10
  (b) Less than 10

4 Join the dots from 1 to 66 and find the hidden bird.

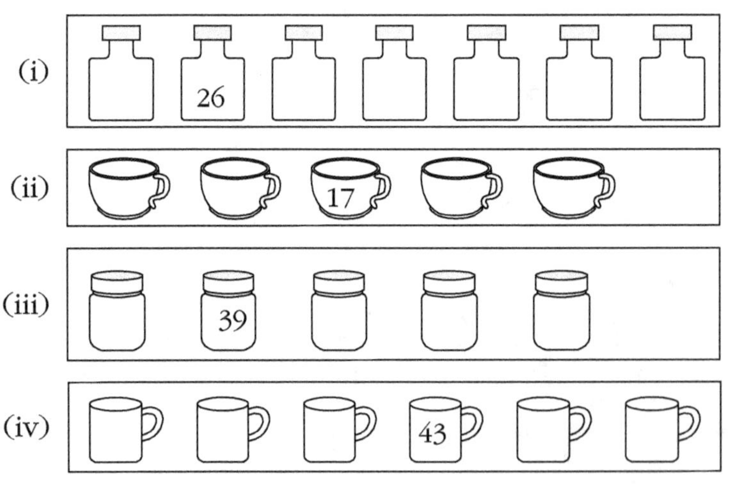

5 Sumedha marked numbers on different jars and mugs; she had in her kitchen and arranged them in an order on a shelf. But the numbers on some jars disappeared. Write the correct number on each jar and mug.

(i)

(ii)

(iii)

(iv)

6 **Fill the missing numbers.**

(i) 15, 16, ______, ______, ______, ______, ______, ______, ______, 24

(ii) 56, ______, ______, ______, 60, ______, ______, ______, ______

(iii) 32, ______, 34, ______, ______, ______, ______, 39, ______

(iv) 88, ______, ______, ______, ______, ______, ______, ______, 96

(v) 45, ______, 47, ______, ______, ______, ______, ______, 53

(vi) ______, ______, ______, ______, ______, ______, 46, ______

(vii) ______, ______, 72, ______, ______, 75, ______, ______

7 **There are nine persons standing in a line.**

(i) Write the name of the person standing on the following positions.

(a) Sixth position ____________   (b) Ninth position ____________

(c) Third position ____________   (d) Sidra is ________ position in the line.

(e) Katica is on the ____________ position.

(ii) How many girls are standing in the line? ____________

(iii) Find the total number of persons standing in the line. ____________

(iv) How many persons are standing before the Katica? ____________

8 **Fill in the blanks.**

(i) The position of V in the word HEAVIER is _____________

(ii) The position of G in the word BAG is _____________

(iii) The position of S in the word THURSDAY is _____________

(iv) The position of E in the word PENCIL is _____________

9 **Find the numbers that comes after, before or in between the given numbers and match the following. One has been done for you.**

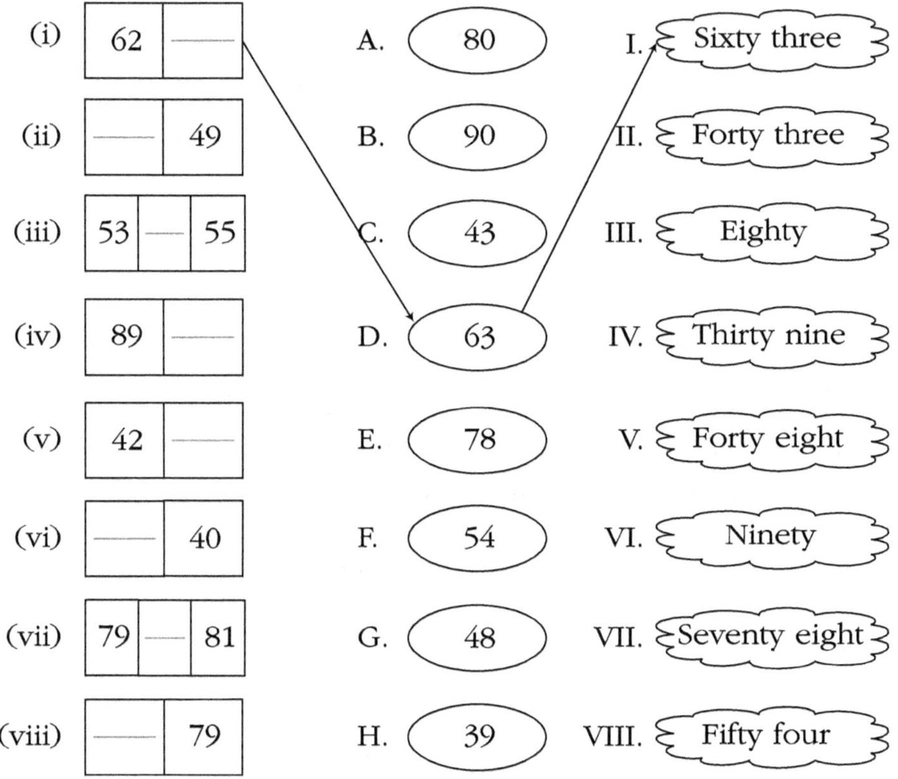

How Much Can You Carry?

1 Tick (✓) the object in each part which is heavier in weight. One has been done for you.

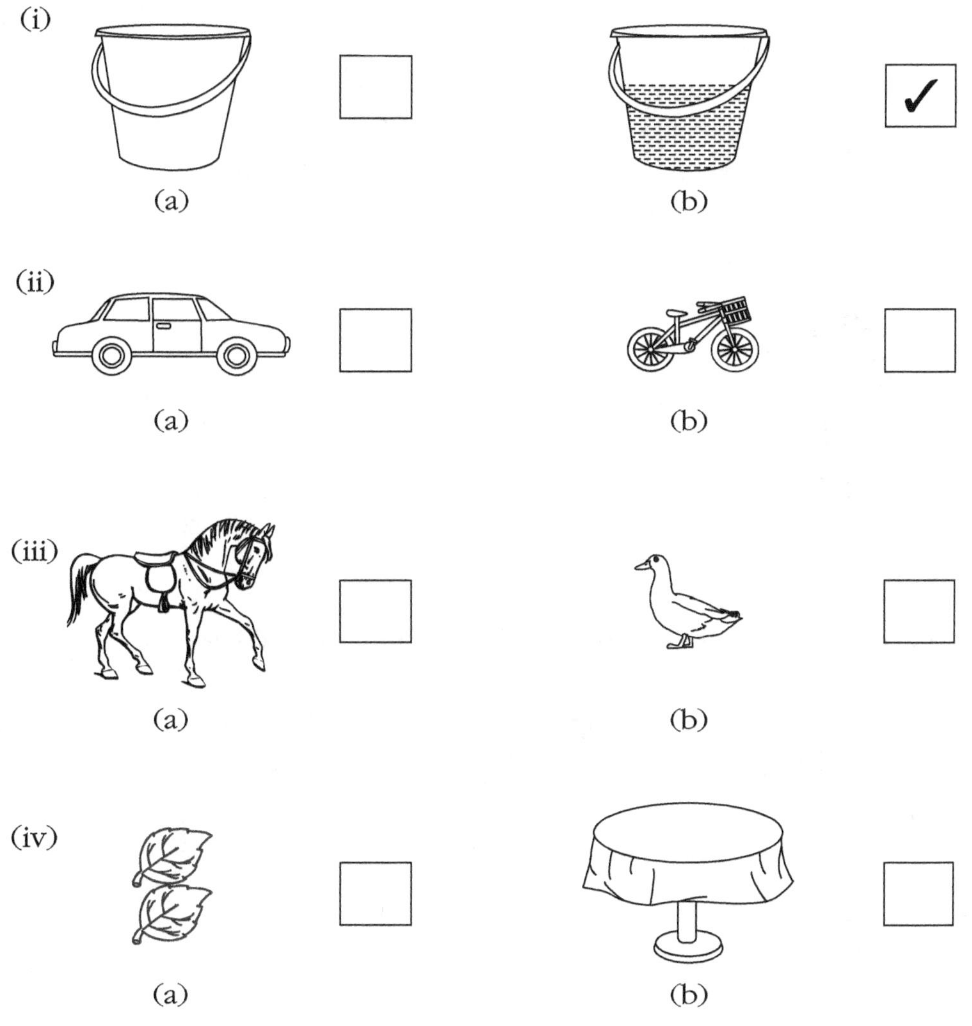

(i)
(a)
(b)

(ii)
(a)
(b)

(iii)
(a)
(b)

(iv)
(a)
(b)

2 Tick (✓) the object in each part which is lighter in weight.

(i)

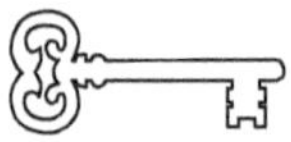

(a)   (b)

(ii)

(a)   (b)

(iii)

(a)   (b)

(iv)

(a)   (b)

3 Tick (✓) the heavier side and cross (✗) the lighter side.

(i)

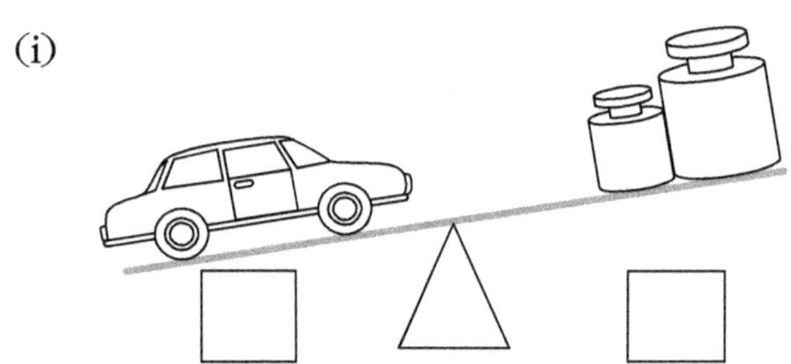

(ii)

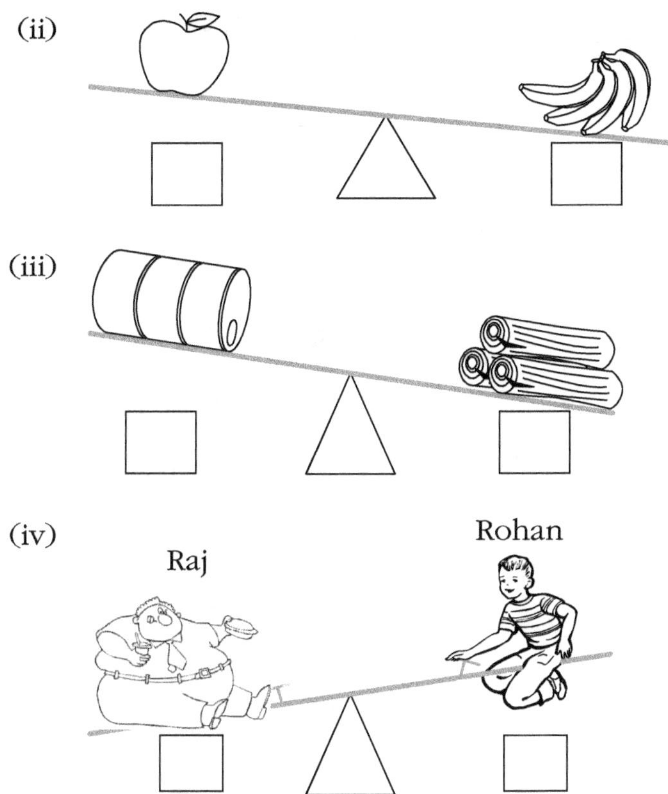

(iii)

(iv) Raj   Rohan

4 Study the diagrams given below and fill in the blanks accordingly.

(i)

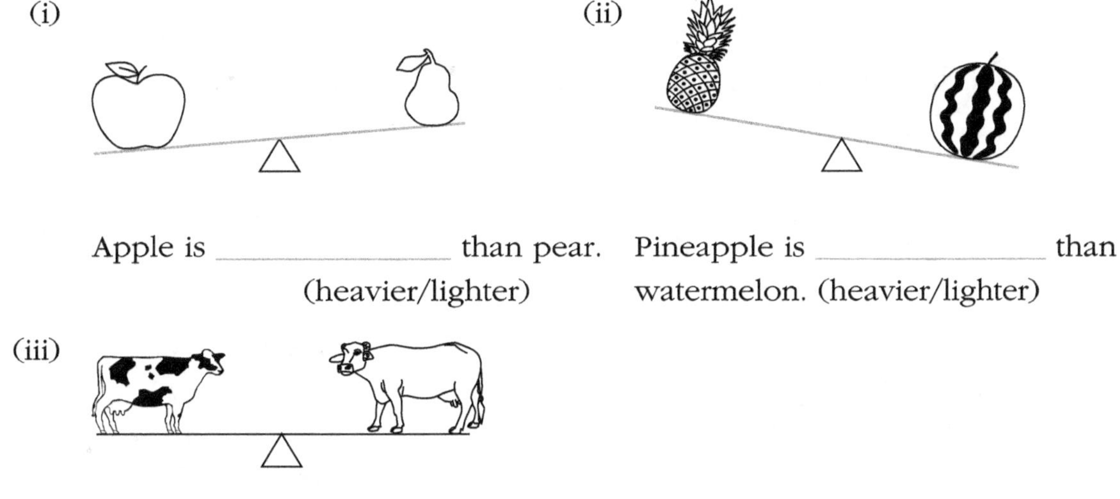

(ii)

Apple is _______________ than pear.
(heavier/lighter)

Pineapple is _______________ than watermelon. (heavier/lighter)

(iii)

Cow and buffalo have _______________ weight. (equal/unequal)

5 Place the objects on the weighing scale by drawing lines. One has been done for you.

(i)

(a)   (b)

(ii)

(a)   (b)

(iii)

SACK of RICE

(a)   (b)

(iv)

(a)   (b)

6 Circle the object which can be used to measure the weight.

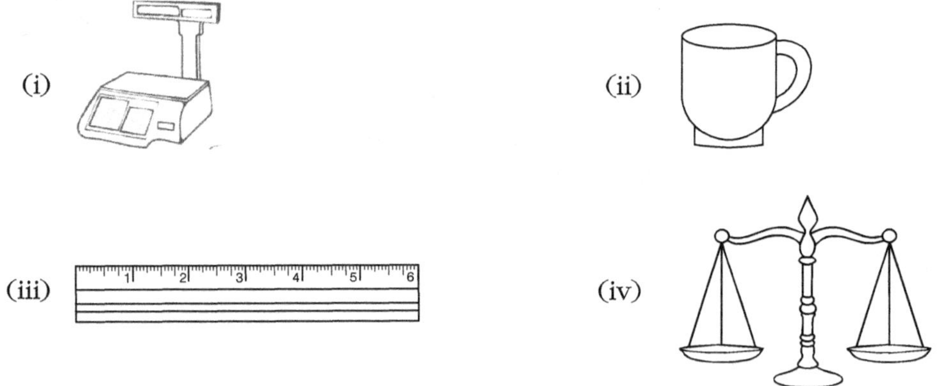

(i)

(ii)

(iii)

(iv)

7 Match the picture of the animal with the thing it can carry.

(i)    (a) 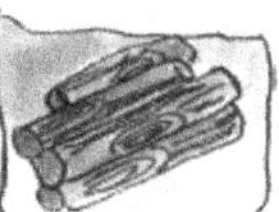

(ii)    (b) 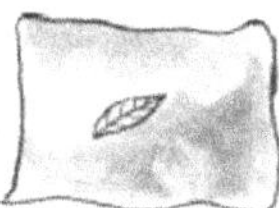

(iii)    (c) 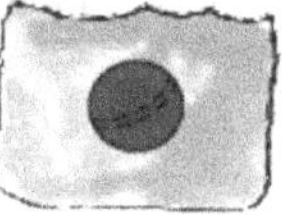

8   I. Find how much each object weighs? One has been done for you.

(i) 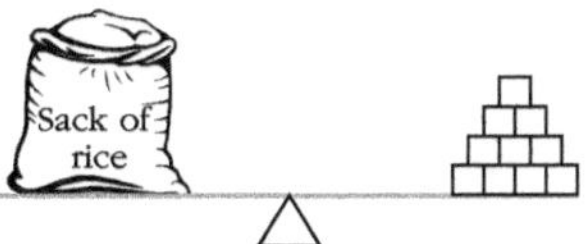

A sack of rice weighs <u>10</u> blocks.

(ii) 

A bag weighs _________ blocks.

(iii) 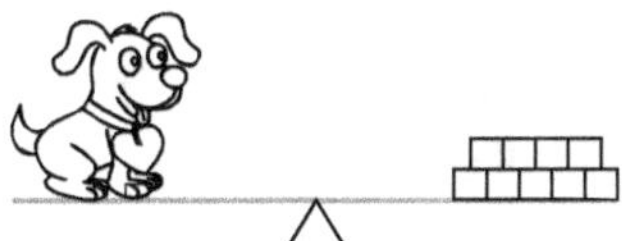

A puppy weighs _______ blocks.

(iv) 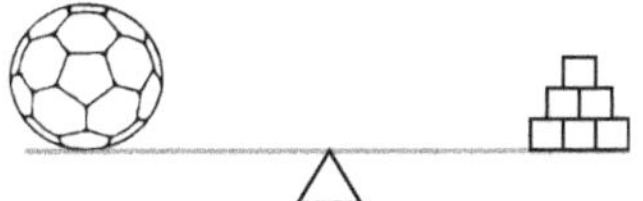

A ball weighs _______ blocks.

9 The weights of four objects are given below.

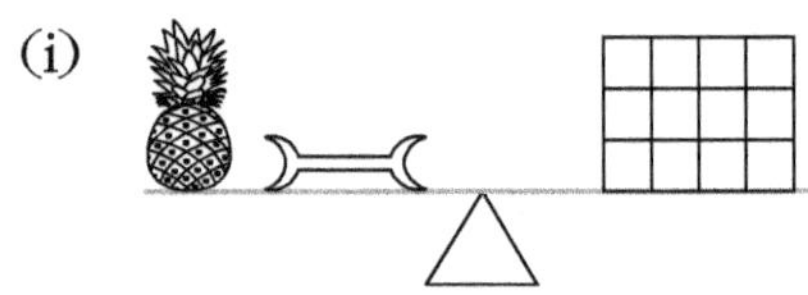 , 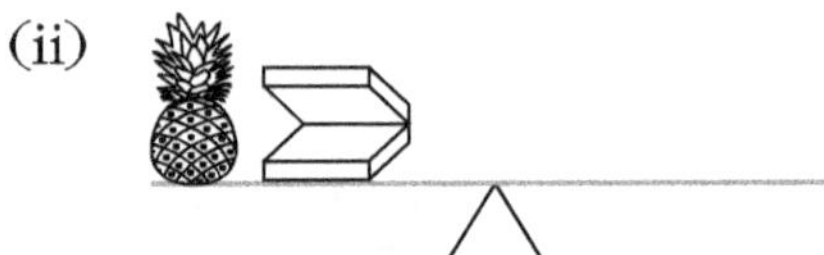

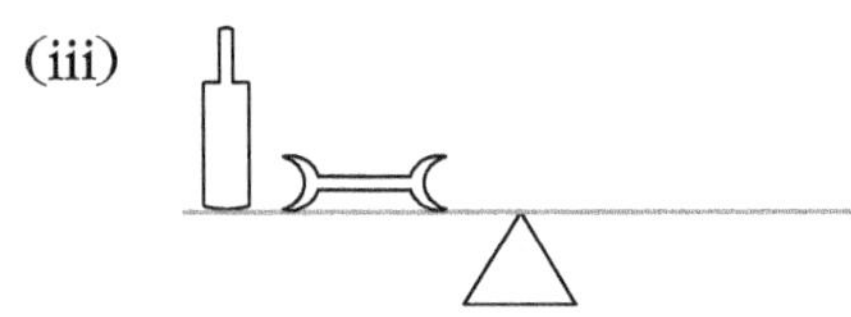 , 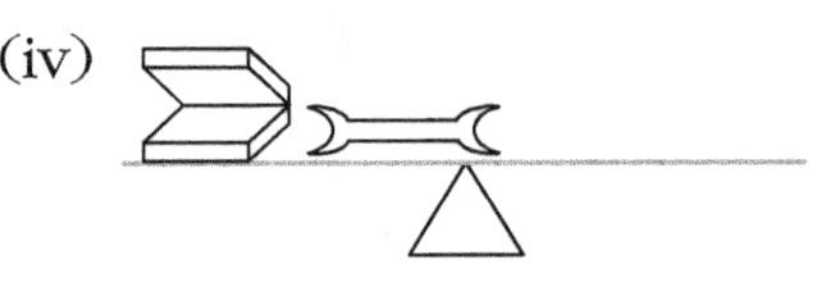

Draw the correct number of blocks to make both sides equal. One has been done for you.

(i)

(ii)

(iii)

(iv)

Counting in Tens

1 Answer the following questions.

(i) How many boxes of 10 apples are there? _________

(ii) How many apples are there in all boxes? _________

(iii) How many apples are out of the boxes? _________

(iv) There are _______ + 7 = _______ apples.

2 Calculate quickly.

Radha made a bouquet of 10 flowers for her friend.

(i) How many flowers are used in 5 such bouquets?

(ii) How many flowers are required to make 7 such bouquets?

(iii) 9 bouquets will have _________ flowers.

(iv) 40 flowers will be used in _________ bouquets.

3 Solomon likes to play with balloons. He purchased some bunches of balloons as shown below.

     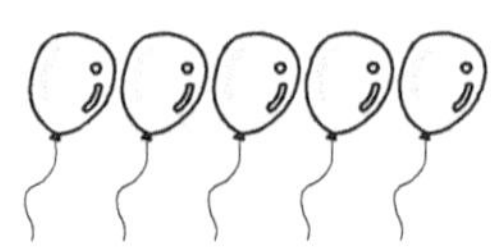

Now, fill in the blanks.

(i) There are _____________ bunches of balloons.

(ii) Each bunch consists of _________ balloons.

(iii) The number of loose balloons is _________.

(iv) There are _________ balloons in all.

(v) 4 such bunches will have _________ balloons.

4 Circle the groups of ten and fill in the boxes. One has been done for you.

(i) 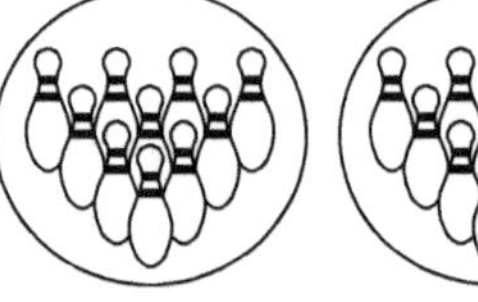 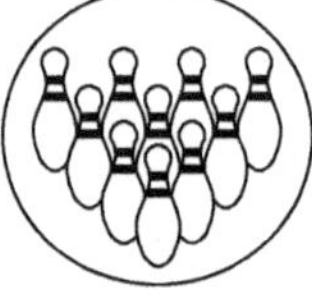 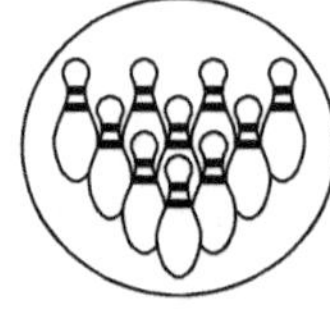 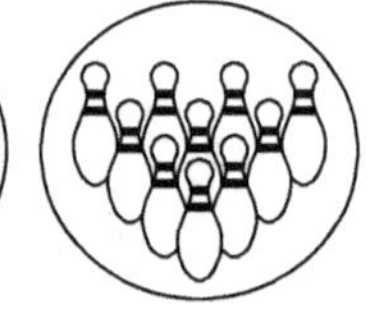

Groups of ten	Loose bottles
4	3

The number is <u>43</u>.

(ii)    

Groups of ten	Loose birds

The number is ______.

(iii) 

Groups of ten	Loose flowers

The number is ______.

5 Tick (✓) the pattern which shows the correct number given below.

(i) 63

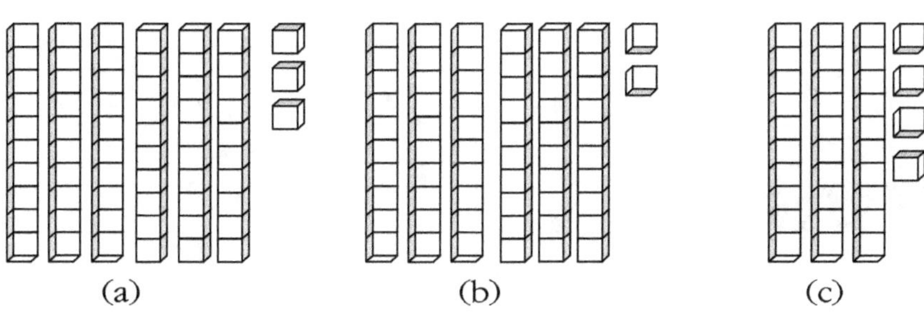

(a)   (b)   (c)

(ii) 29

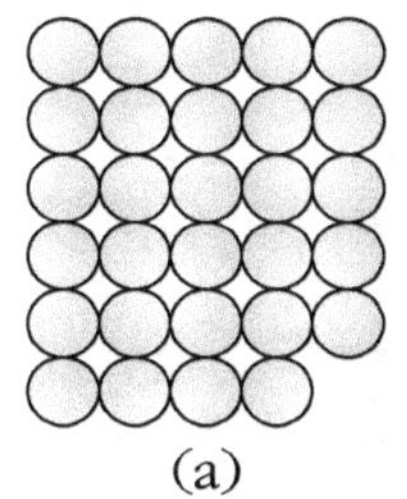

(a)

(b)

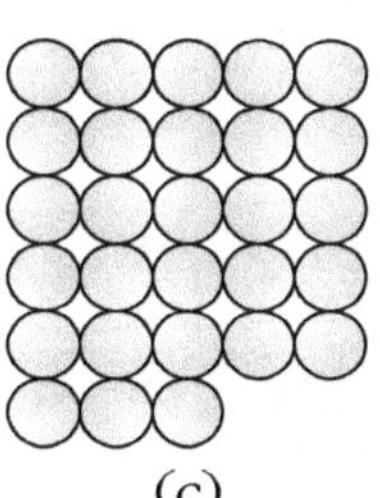

(c)

6 Cody collected some cards. Each card has $3 + 4 + 3$ flowers.

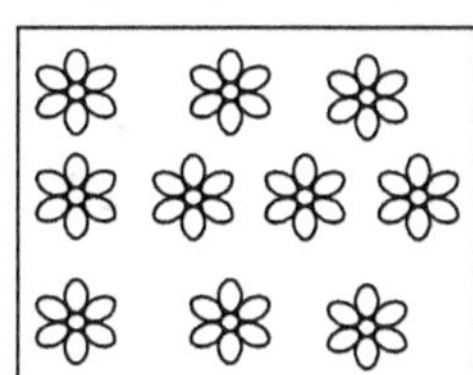 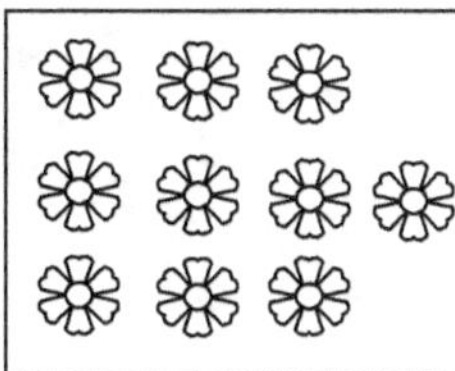  

(i) How many cards did Cody collect in all? ______________

(ii) How many flowers are there in all cards? ______________

(iii) Draw 4 flowers on each card given below in a different way.

Patterns

1 Rohan's grandmother is making beautiful design patterns on mats and bedsheets. Help her in completing the patterns.

(i) 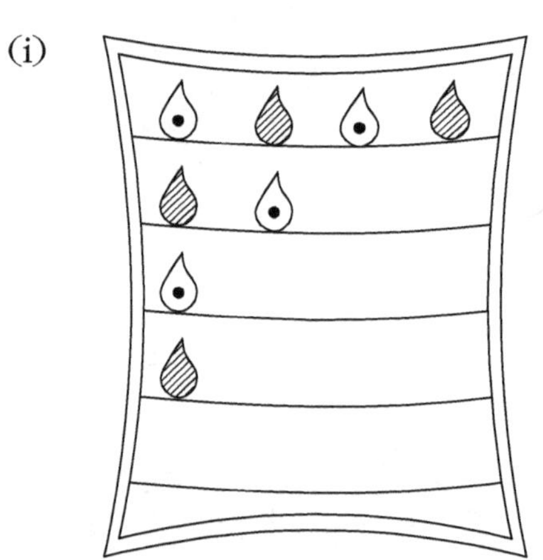

(ii) 

(iii) 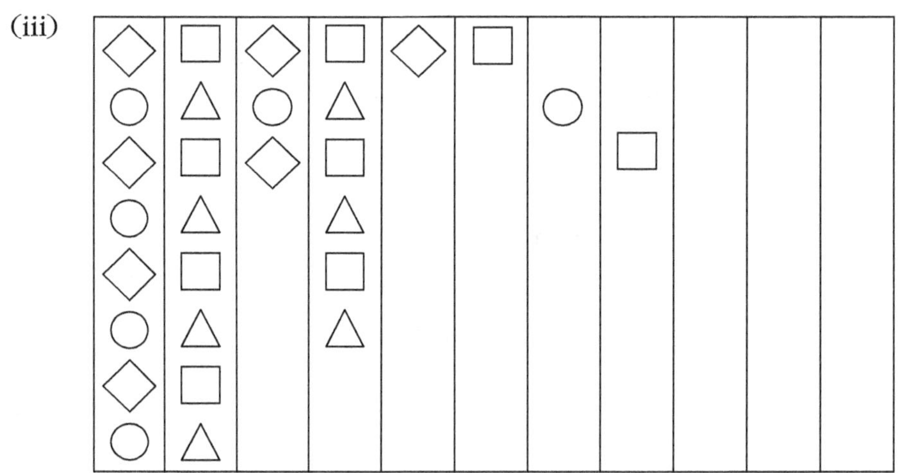

2 Aaru has decorated a saree of her mother using some patterns of blocks. A part of each pattern is missing. Complete the missing part on the saree.

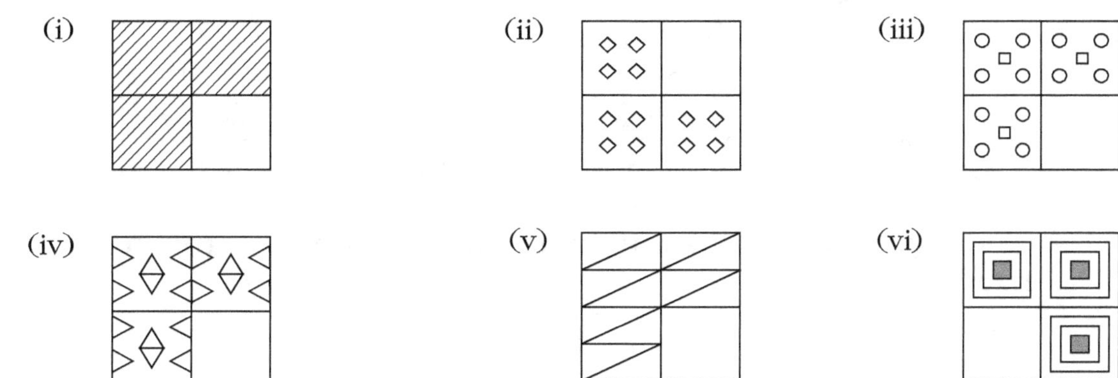

3 Rupa's brother torn away the pages of her design book from a corner. Choose the option which is the correct torn part of the design.

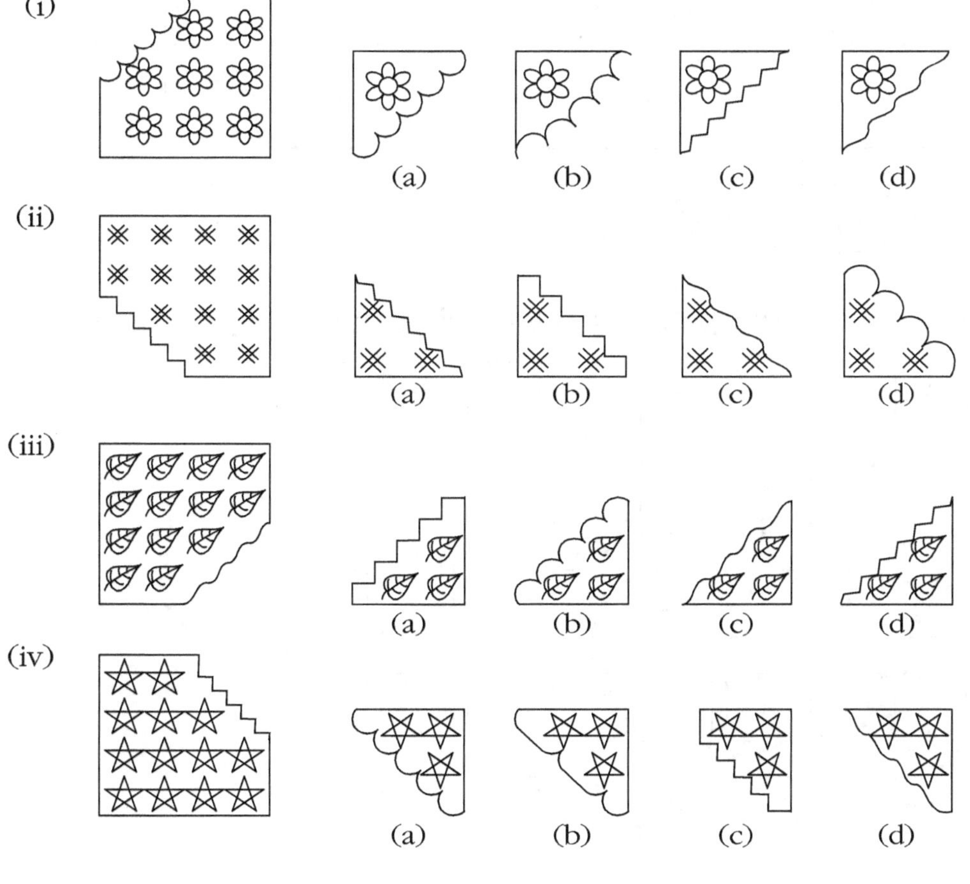

4 Ankita wants to make a pattern of necklace using beads given below. Can you guess which of these cannot be formed?

(a)   (b)   (c)   (d)

5 Study the following patterns carefully and complete the missing figures.

(i)

(ii)

(iii)

(iv)

(v)

6 Identify the number patterns given below and fill up the boxes.

(i)

| 2 | 4 | 6 | 8 | | | | |

(ii)

| 25 | 26 | 27 | 28 | | | | |

(iii)

| 33 | 36 | 39 | 42 | | | | |

(iv)

| 28 | 38 | 48 | 58 | | | | |

(v)

| 10 | 15 | 20 | 25 | | | | |

7 Find the next terms of the given pattern.

8 A monkey jumps and goes on every 8th number. Write the next numbers on which the monkey will jump.

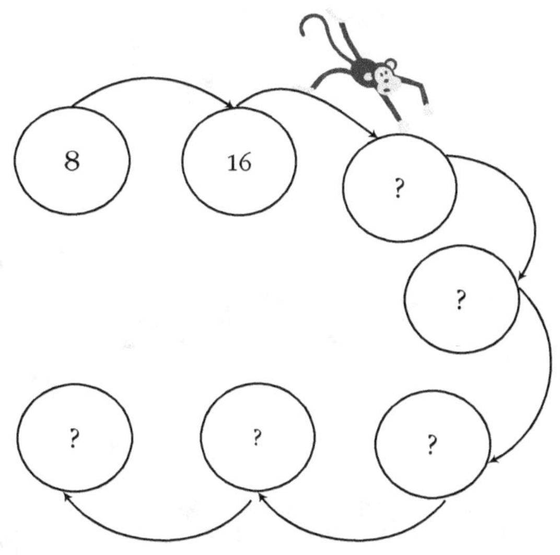

Footprints

1 Guess and match the animals/birds with their footprints.

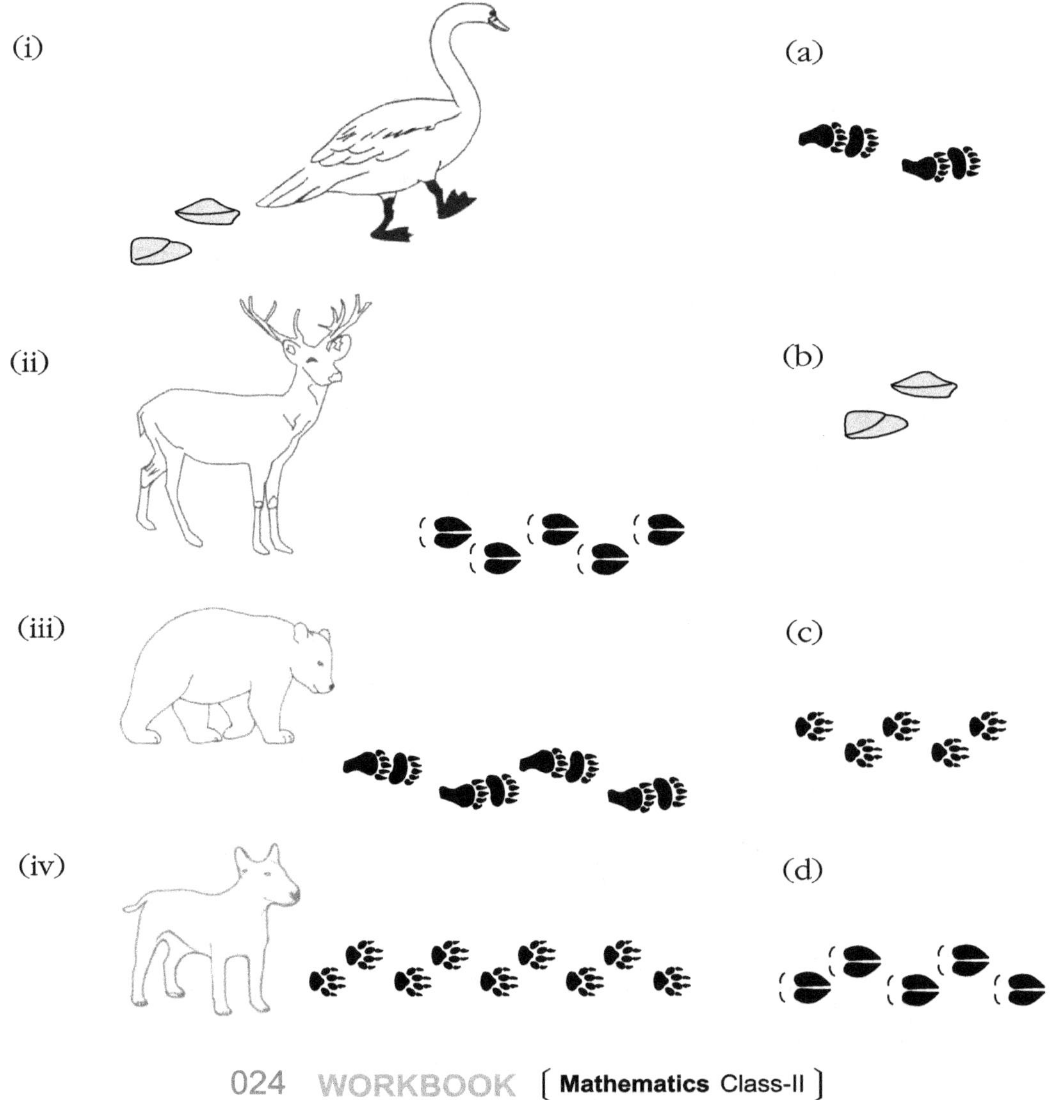

2 Match the objects of Column I with its correct tracing in Column II. One has been done for you.

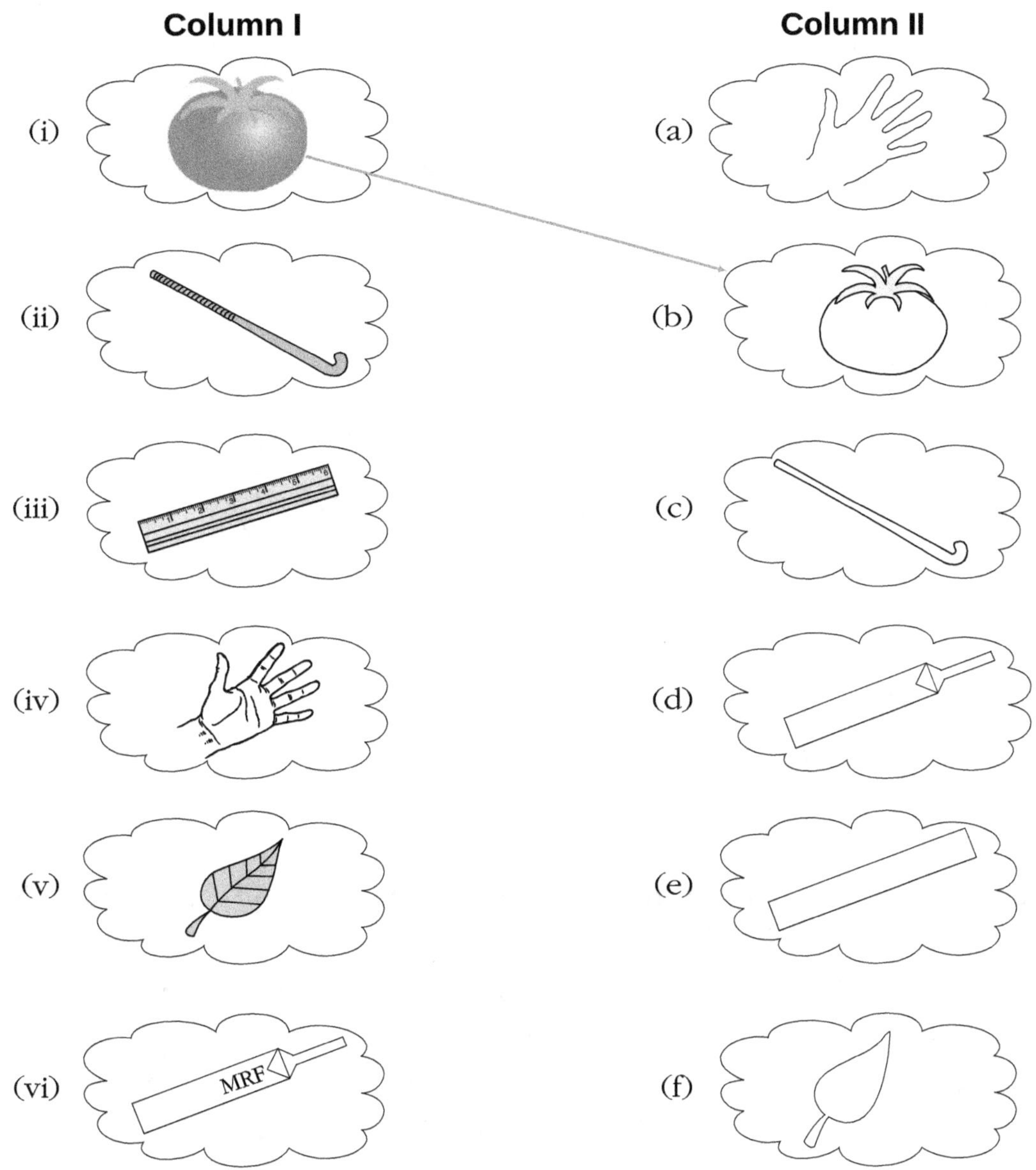

3 Complete the pictures given on the right by drawing the same pictures given on the left.

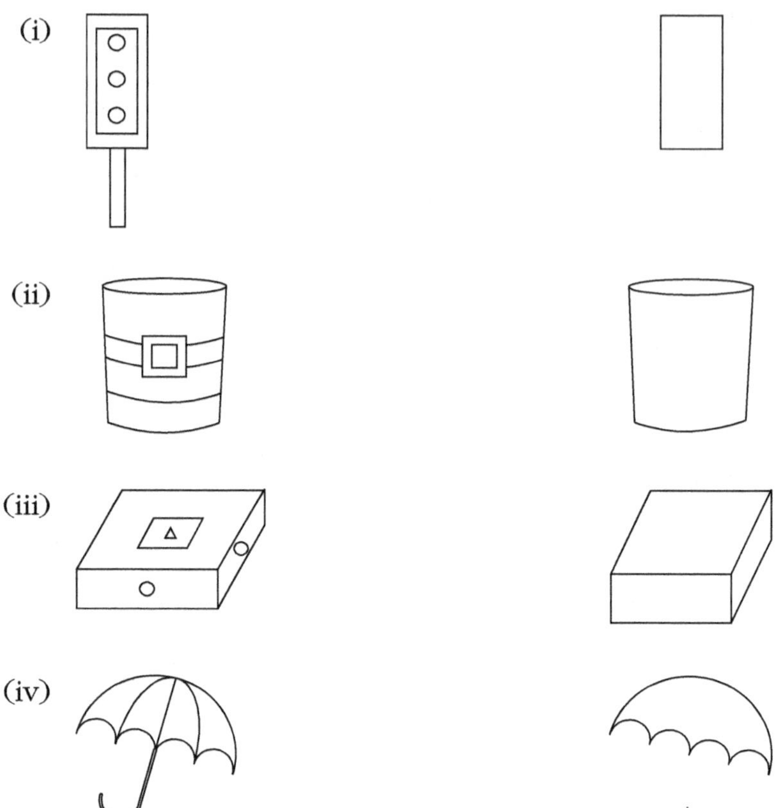

(i)

(ii)

(iii)

(iv)

4 Arrange the following things in the correct column of the table given below according to its trace.

	 ○	▭ ▢ ◇	△
(i)			
(ii)			
(iii)			
(iv)			

5 Priya draw the following picture in her notebook using different shapes.

Observe the picture and answer the questions.

(i) The number of triangles △ are _____________ .

(ii) The number of circles ○ are _____________ .

(iii) The number of squares ▢ are _____________ .

(iv) The number of rectangles ▭ are _____________ .

Jugs and Mugs

1 Count the objects you can use to measure the amount of liquid and write below.

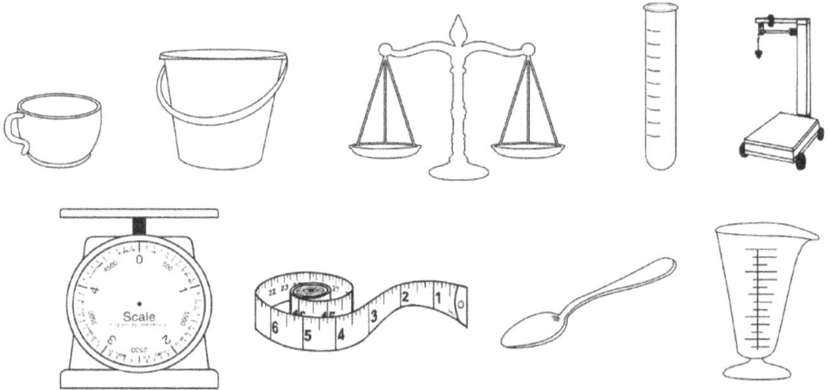

The number of objects to measure the capacity of liquid are ___________.

2 Circle the lemons that are needed to make given glasses of lemon drink. One has been done for you.

two glasses of lemon drink need ⬭ one lemon.

(i)   ∪∪∪∪∪∪∪∪   =   ◯◯◯◯◯

(ii)   ∪∪∪∪∪∪   =   ◯◯◯◯◯

(iii)   ∪∪∪∪∪∪∪∪∪∪   =   ◯◯◯◯◯◯◯◯◯◯

(iv)   ∪∪∪∪∪∪∪
∪∪∪∪∪∪∪   =   ◯◯◯◯◯◯◯◯◯◯◯◯◯◯

3 Study the given information and answer the questions.

Each 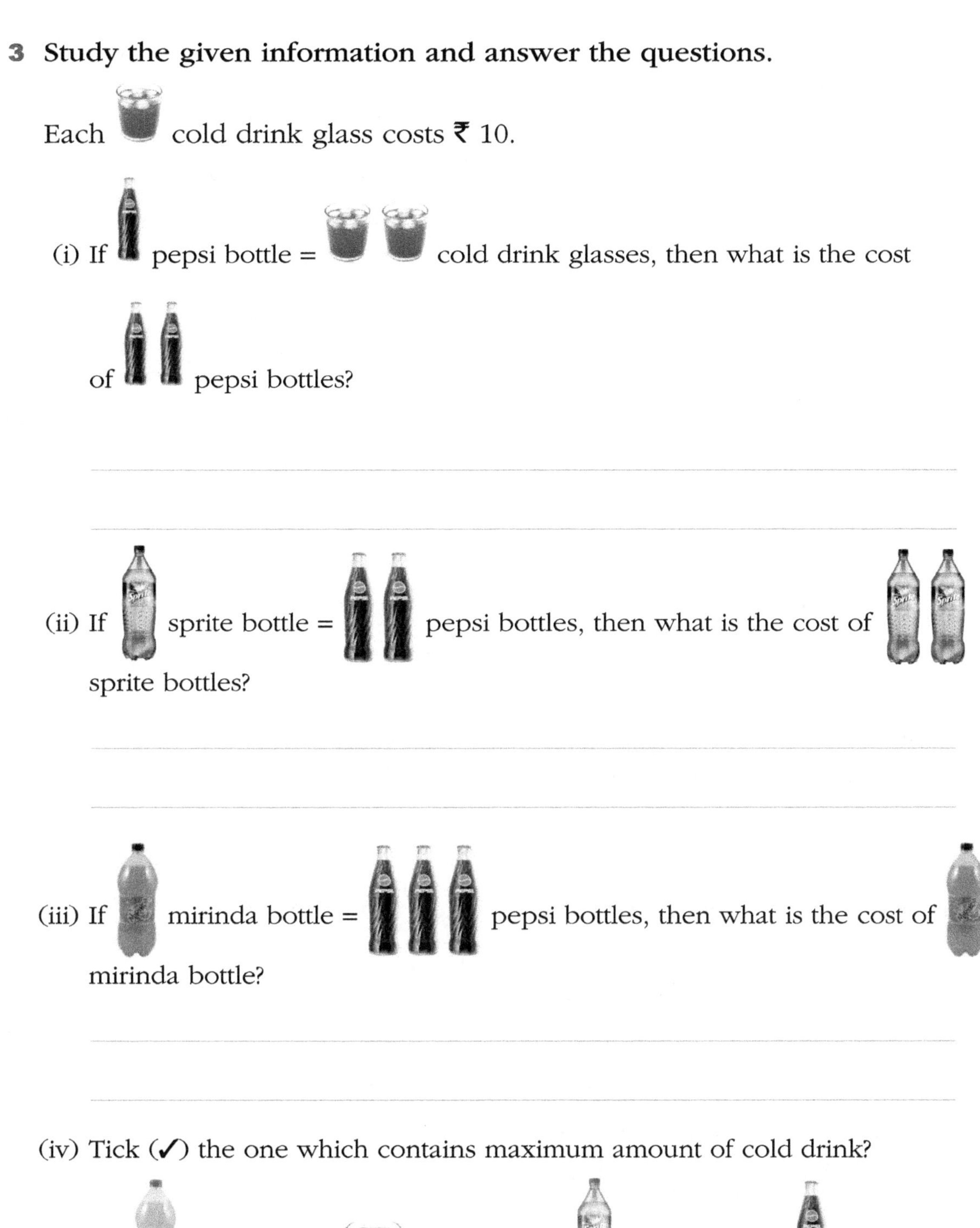 cold drink glass costs ₹ 10.

(i) If [pepsi bottle] pepsi bottle = [cold drink glasses] cold drink glasses, then what is the cost of [pepsi bottles] pepsi bottles?

____

____

(ii) If [sprite bottle] sprite bottle = [pepsi bottles] pepsi bottles, then what is the cost of [sprite bottles] sprite bottles?

____

____

(iii) If [mirinda bottle] mirinda bottle = [pepsi bottles] pepsi bottles, then what is the cost of [mirinda bottle] mirinda bottle?

____

____

(iv) Tick (✓) the one which contains maximum amount of cold drink?

(a)   (b)   (c)   (d)

4 Look at the following pictures carefully and answer the given questions.

| Jug | Dropper | Bottle | Bucket | Cup |

(i) Which contains the least amount of liquid (capacity)?

____

____

(ii) Which contains the most amount of liquid (capacity)?

____

____

(iii) Which container do you use to drink tea?

____

____

(iv) Arrange the containers in the order of the amount of liquid they can hold liquid (capacity) starting from the smallest.

____

____

5 Study the following information and answer the questions.

mug = glasses

and bucket = mugs

(i) Which container holds the least water? ___________ (1 mug/1 glass/1 bucket)

(ii) How many glasses of water will fill 1 bucket? ___________ (24 glasses/ 23 glasses /20 glasses)

6 **Word problems.**

   (i) A cow can drink 2 buckets of water at once. How many buckets of water can 2 cows drink at once?

   (ii) Amelia needs 4 buckets of water to complete all the household work in 1 day. How many buckets of water will she need in 4 days?

   (iii) If a balloon needs 3 cups of water to fill, then how many cups of water will be needed to fill 3 balloons?

   (iv) Shaily uses 6 glasses of water to make 1 jug of juice. How many glasses will she use to make 3 jugs of juice?

Chapter 8

Tens and Ones

1 Draw ₹ 10 notes and ₹ 1 coins that you will need to pay for the given purchased objects. One has been done for you.

(i) ₹ 53 

₹ 10	₹ 1
↓	↓
5	3

(ii) ₹ 95  __________

(iii) ₹ 67  __________

(iv) ₹ 28 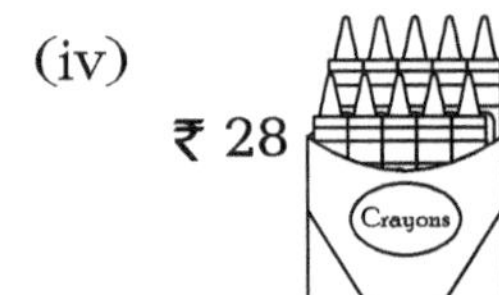 __________

(v) ₹ 37  __________

(vi) ₹ 12  __________

2 Write down how many ₹ 10 notes and ₹ 1 coins will you need to buy the following things? One has been done for you.

(i) 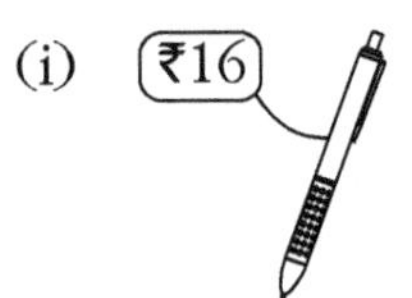

(a) $10 + 1 + 1 + 1 + 1 + 1 + 1$

(b) One ₹ 10 note and 6 ₹ 1 coins

(ii) 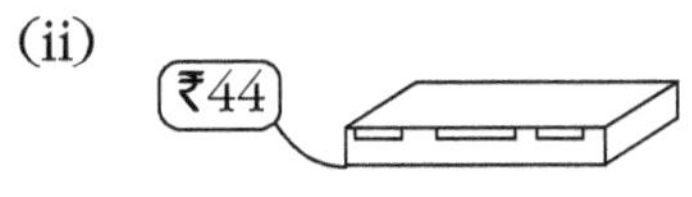

(a) ______________________________

(b) ______________________________

(iii) 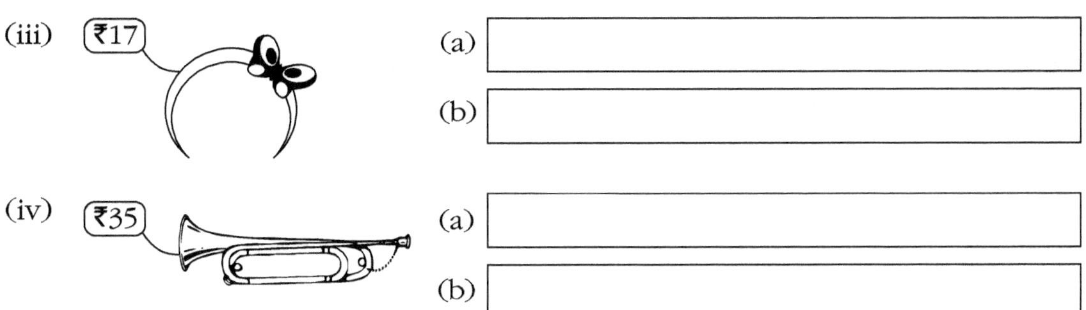 ₹17   (a)

(b)

(iv) ₹35   (a)

(b)

3 Write the total sum of money. One has been done for you.

(i) 

$$30 + 4 = ₹\ 34$$

(ii) 

(iii) 

(iv)

____

(v)

____

4 **Fill in the blanks. One has been done for you.**

(i) $32 = \underline{30} + \underline{2}$

(ii) $97 = \underline{\hspace{2cm}} + \underline{\hspace{2cm}}$

(iii) $65 = \underline{\hspace{2cm}} + 5$

(iv) $\underline{\hspace{2cm}} = 20 + 9$

(v) $83 = \underline{\hspace{2cm}} + \underline{\hspace{2cm}}$

(vi) $92 = 90 + \underline{\hspace{2cm}}$

(vii) $58 = \underline{\hspace{2cm}} + \underline{\hspace{2cm}}$

(viii) $28 = \underline{\hspace{2cm}} + 8$

(ix) $69 = \underline{\hspace{2cm}} + \underline{\hspace{2cm}}$

(x) $82 = \underline{\hspace{2cm}} + \underline{\hspace{2cm}}$

5 5 friends went to a mela and played a game of rings to collect money. The ring thrown by each one is given in the following diagram. Answer the following questions on the basis of given diagram.

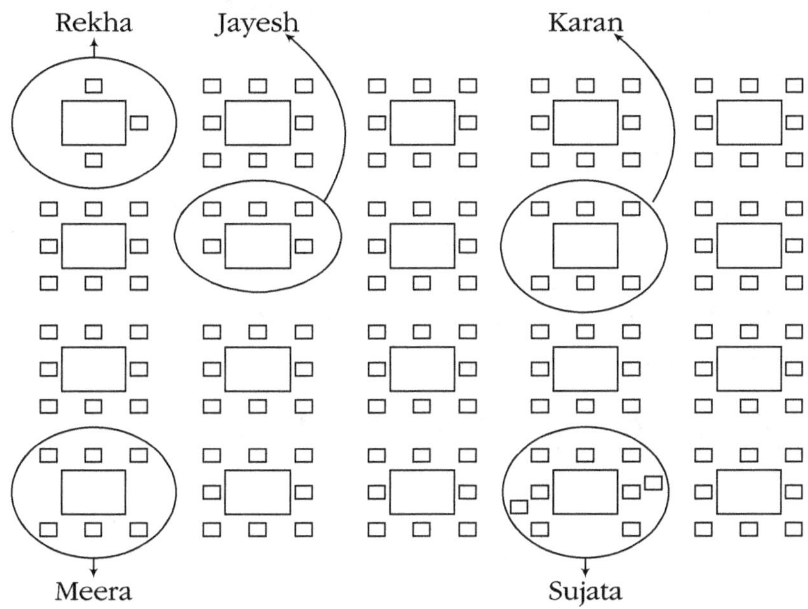

(i) If ☐ = ₹ 10 and ☐ = ₹ 1, then fill the table with the amount of money each won.

	Name	Money (in ₹)
(a)	Rekha	
(b)	Meera	
(c)	Jayesh	
(d)	Karan	
(e)	Sujata	

(ii) Who won the maximum amount of money? __________

(iii) Who won the minimum amount of money? __________

(iv) Who won the same amount of money? __________

6 Some numbers are given below. Break the numbers and represent them using dots. One has been done for you.

(i) 24 = 20 + 4

(ii) 23 = _______ + _______

(iii) 18 = _______ + _______

(iv) 26 = _______ + _______

7 If ▲ = 10 cards and ■ = 1 card, draw the cards representing the given numbers. One has been done for you.

(i) 28 = ▲ ▲ ■ ■ ■ ■ ■ ■ ■ ■

(ii) 53 = _______

(iii) 32 = _______

(iv) 86 = _______

(v) 97 = _______

(vi) 30 = _______

(vii) 73 = _______

8 Ella has bought some beads to make necklace. Each necklace will consist of 10 beads. Find how many necklaces can be made, if she has the given number of beads. One has been done for you.

Number of beads	Number of necklaces	Beads left
(i) 23	2	3
(ii) 48		
(iii) 63		
(iv) 75		
(v) 87		

9 Students of some classes decided to donate some pencils to the 'children's home'. The number of pencils donated by each class is given below.

Class I	78
Class II	65
Class III	59
Class IV	83

The pencils are to be packed in different packets. Each packet contains 10 pencils. Using the above information to fill the table.

	Number of packets made	Number of pencils left
(i) Class I		
(ii) Class II		
(iii) Class III		
(iv) Class IV		

(v) How many more packets can be made using the pencils left in each class?

Chapter 9

My Funday

1 **Multiple choice questions.**

   (i) The first day of the week is

      (a) Tuesday   ☐   (b) Sunday   ☐

      (c) Monday   ☐   (d) Saturday   ☐

   (ii) The sixth day of the week is

      (a) Saturday   ☐   (b) Monday   ☐

      (c) Sunday   ☐   (d) Tuesday   ☐

   (iii) Which day is funday?

      (a) Thursday   ☐   (b) Sunday   ☐

      (c) Tuesday   ☐   (d) Friday   ☐

   (iv) The fourth day of the week is

      (a) Monday   ☐   (b) Friday   ☐

      (c) Wednesday   ☐   (d) Thursday   ☐

2 **Fill in the blanks.**

   (i) __________ comes before Wednesday.

   (ii) 2 days after Thursday is __________ .

   (iii) If today is Monday, then tomorrow will be __________ .

   (iv) 4 days after Sunday will be __________ .

   (v) 3 days before Tuesday will be __________ .

   (vi) If today is Saturday, then the day before yesterday was __________ .

3 Observe the time table of Class II and answer the following questions.

Period \ Day	Monday	Tuesday	Wednesday	Thursday	Friday	Saturday
Period 1	Maths	English	EVS	English	Hindi	G K
Period 2	Maths	Hindi	Moral Science	Hindi	EVS	Music
Nutrition break						
Period 3	Music	EVS	Computer	GK	Moral Science	Art
Period 4	Library	GK	Maths	Computer	Maths	Library
Nutrition break						
Period 5	English	Maths	Hindi	Maths	Art	Games
Period 6	Hindi	Maths	English	Maths	Art	Games

I. Fill in the blanks. One has been done for you.

	Period	On which days?
(i)	Maths	Monday, Tuesday, Wednesday, Thursday, Friday
(ii)	Music	
(iii)	Library	
(iv)	Hindi	
(v)	English	
(vi)	EVS	
(vii)	GK	
(viii)	Computer	
(ix)	Moral Science	

II. (i) How many nutrition breaks are there each day?

(ii) On which day do the class have Art period?

(iii) On which day do the class have games period?

4 The teachers of Class II decided to give the homework of each subject on some particular days as shown below.

Day	Subject
Monday	Maths, English
Tuesday	Computer, Hindi
Wednesday	English, EVS
Thursday	Maths, Hindi
Friday	EVS, Computer
Saturday	GK, Drawing, Computer

Answer the following questions on the basis of above table.

(i) On which two days homework of Maths will be given?

(ii) On which day homework of GK and Drawing will be given?

(iii) The homework of which subjects will be given on the day after Monday?

(iv) On which day the homework of three subjects will be given?

(v) If today is Wednesday, then homework of which subjects will be given on the day before yesterday?

5 Fill the table with your favourite choice.

	Your favourite	Month in which it comes
Fruit		
Vegetable		
Flower		
Festival		

6 Match the occasion (Column I) to the picture (Column II) and to the month (Column III) in which it comes. One has been done for you.

Column I	Column II	Column III
A. Christmas	(i)	(a) December
B. Gandhi Jayanti	(ii)	(b) October
C. Diwali	(iii)	(c) August
D. Holi	(iv)	(d) March
E. Independence Day	(v)	(e) November

7 State true or false.

(i) January is the seventh month of the year.

(ii) Fourth month of the year is April.

(iii) Fifth day of the week is Friday.

(iv) We use room heaters in summer season.

(v) Kashmir has cold weather.

(vi) Chennai has cold weather.

8 **Fill in the blanks.**

(i) _________ is the first month of the year.

(ii) If this month is May, then next month will be _________.

(iii) The last month of the year is _________.

(iv) _________ comes before October.

(v) _________ and _________ month called the rainy months.

(vi) Tick (✓) the months have 31 days.

(a) January

(b) April

(c) June

(d) October

Chapter 10

Add Our Points

1 **Read the following and answer the questions.**

Robert and Rumena were playing the number maze made in an amusement park as shown below. Rumena starts from number 6 and Robert starts from number 21.

START	8	6	10	13	15
					16
34	30	25	23	21	18
35					
39	40	41	48	49	55
					57
72	70	68	64	61	59
74					
76	81	84	92	96	FINISH 99

(i) If Rumena adds 19 to the number on which she stands, then on which number will she reach?

(ii) If Robert adds 18 to the number where he stands, then on which number will he reach?

____

(iii) Which number should Rumena add to 25 to reach number 41?

$\boxed{} + \boxed{25} = \boxed{41}$

(iv) Which number should Robert add to 39 to be just ahead of Rumena?

$\boxed{39} + \boxed{} = \boxed{48}$

(v) Which numbers should Rumena and Robert need to add to reach the finish number box?

Rumena (a) $\boxed{} + \boxed{41} = \boxed{99}$

Robert (b) $\boxed{} + \boxed{48} = \boxed{99}$

2 Fill in the missing numbers.

(i) $5 + 15 = \boxed{}$

(ii) $8 + 11 = \boxed{}$

(iii) $5 + 19 = \boxed{}$

(iv) $6 + 15 = \boxed{}$

(v) $\boxed{} + 33 = 44$

(vi) $18 + \boxed{} = 24$

(vii) $19 + 21 = \boxed{}$

(viii) $19 + 12 = \boxed{}$

3 Study the figure given below and tick (✓) the correct option.

(i) What is the total weight of all the vegetables?

(a) 12 kg $\boxed{}$

(b) 8 kg $\boxed{}$

(c) 14 kg $\boxed{}$

(d) 13 kg $\boxed{}$

(ii) If Sarah can carry only 7 kg weight at a time, then which of the following two vegetables will she purchase?

    (a) Cauliflower and onions

    (b) Potatoes and onions

    (c) Cauliflower and potatoes

    (d) Either (a) or (b)

(iii) The total weight of potatoes and onions is

    (a) 7 kg   (b) 11 kg

    (c) 14 kg   (d) None of these

4 Fill in the blanks.

(i) ₹ 100 = __________ ₹ 50 notes.   (ii) ₹ 500 = __________ ₹ 100 notes.

(iii) ₹ 50 = __________ ₹ 10 notes.   (iv) ₹ 100 = __________ ₹ 20 notes.

(v) ₹ 20 = __________ ₹ 5 coins.

5 Adding money.

Ashi has the following currency notes with her.

Write the notes or coins which she use to pay for the following items. [she can use only two currencies at a time]. One has been done for you.

(i)

    ₹ 25   One ₹ 20 note and one ₹ 5 coin

(ii)

    ₹ 30

(iii) 

₹ 3 ____________________________________

(iv) 

₹ 15 ____________________________________

6 How much is the cost of each object?

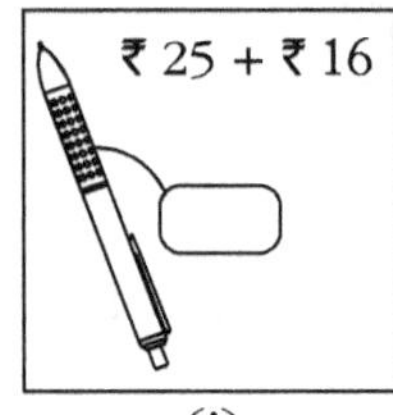

₹ 25 + ₹ 16

(i)

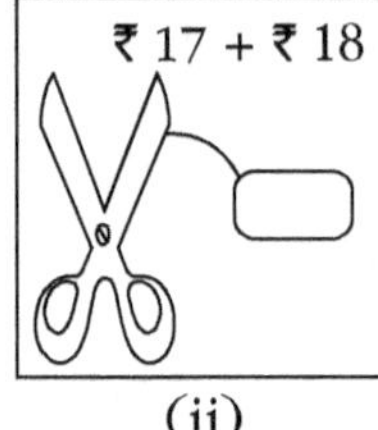

₹ 17 + ₹ 18

(ii)

₹ 14 + ₹ 19

(iii)

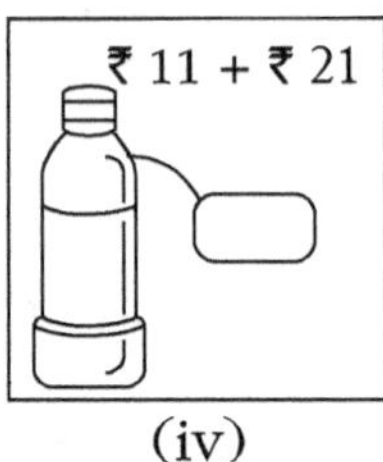

₹ 11 + ₹ 21

(iv)

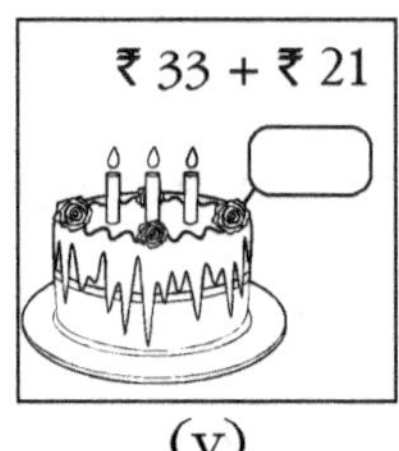

₹ 33 + ₹ 21

(v)

7 Find the sum of the given numbers. One has been done for you.

(i) 4 + 7 + 8 = 19
(11)

(ii) 8 + 9 + 6 = ____________

(iii) 5 + 8 + 2 = ____________

(iv) 9 + 8 + 7 = ____________

(v) 8 + 4 + 2 = ____________

(vi) 7 + 7 + 7 = ____________

(vii) 2 + 5 + 9 = ____________

8 Fill the circles by adding the numbers given in the rows and columns (across and down). One has been done for you.

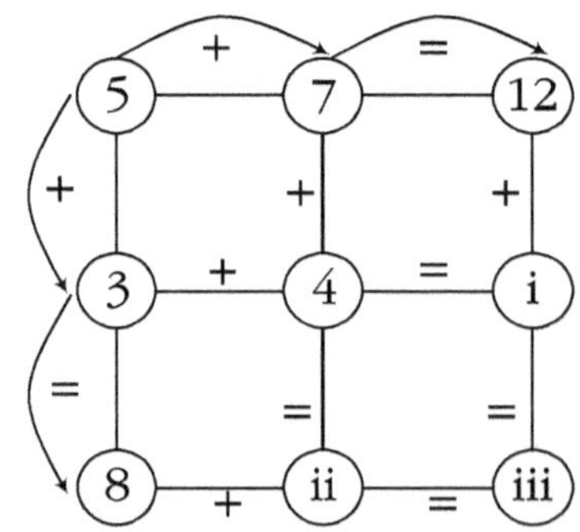

9 Four friends are skipping the rope in a playground. Add the numbers given below them to get the total number of times they skipped the rope. Then, answer the questions that follows.

(i) Who skips the rope minimum number of times?

____

(ii) Who skips the rope 38 times?

____

(iii) How many times Sachin and Reena together skip the rope?

____

(iv) Who won the game?

____

10 In each of the following, write the correct weight to balance each scale. One has been done for you.

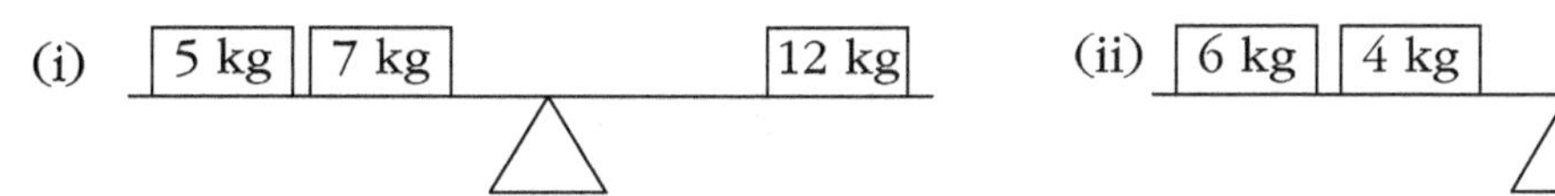

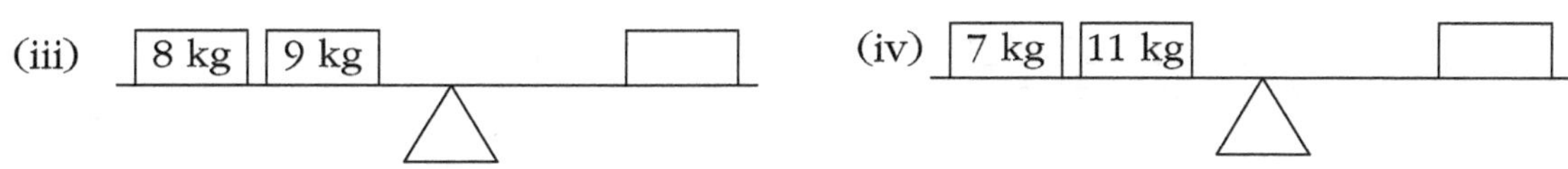

Lines and Lines

1 Classify the following objects as standing, slanting, sleeping or curved.

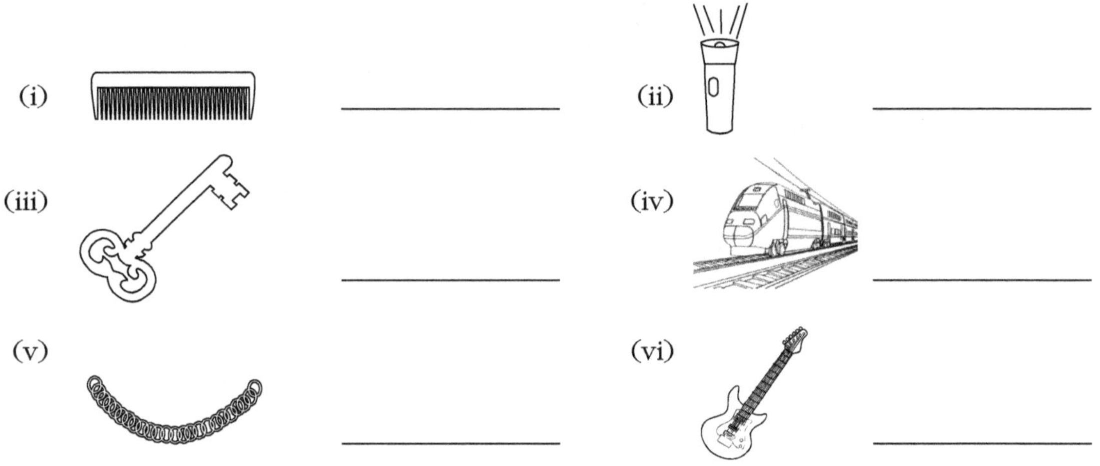

(i)   ________________

(ii)   ________________

(iii)   ________________

(iv)   ________________

(v)   ________________

(vi)   ________________

2 Match the objects of Column I with the correct type of line in Column II.

Column I   **Column II**

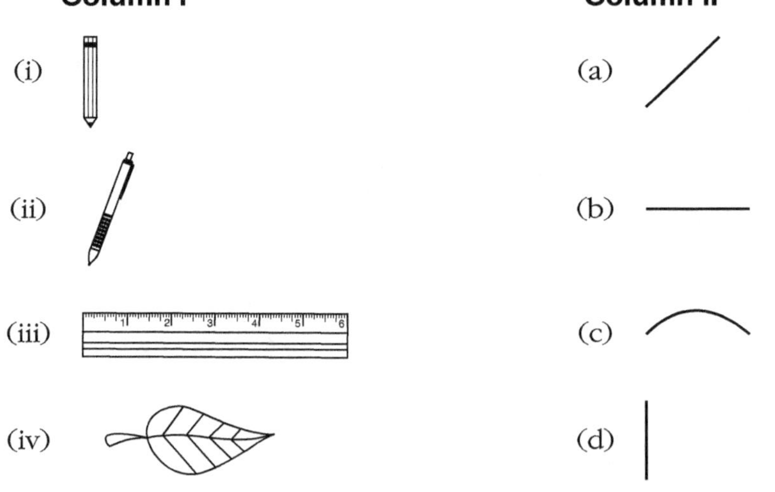

(i)

(ii)

(iii)

(iv)

(a)

(b)

(c)

(d)

3 Tick (✓) the patterns that are made up of straight lines and cross (✗) the patterns that are made up of curved lines.

(i) 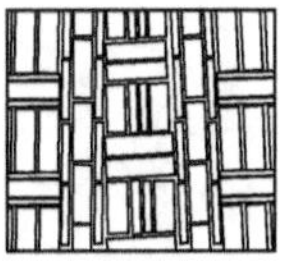 (ii)  (iii)

(iv)  (v)  (vi)

4 Count the number of lines in the given words.

(i)

PEACOCK

(a) Standing lines _________
(b) Sleeping lines _________

(ii)

INDIA

(a) Standing lines _________

(b) Sleeping lines _________

(iii)

(a) Standing lines   ________________

(b) Sleeping lines   ________________

5 Saina made this drawing card for her best friend. Count the number of straight lines and curved lines used in the card.

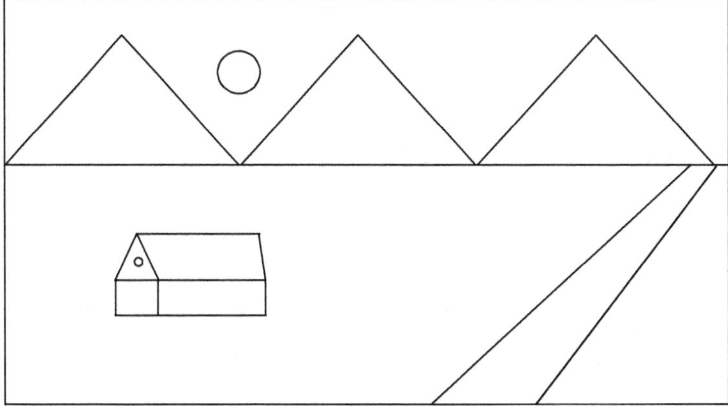

(i) Straight lines   [ ]

(ii) Curved lines   [ ]

6 Make some pictures by joining the dots using straight and curved lines. One has been done for you.

How many pictures have you drawn?

7 Maya drew a picture using slanting, standing and sleeping lines. Count the number of lines used.

(i) Standing lines ________________

(ii) Sleeping lines ________________

(iii) Slanting lines ________________

8 Count the number of standing, sleeping and curved lines in each figure.

(i) 

Standing lines   = __________

Sleeping lines   = __________

Curved lines   = __________

(ii) 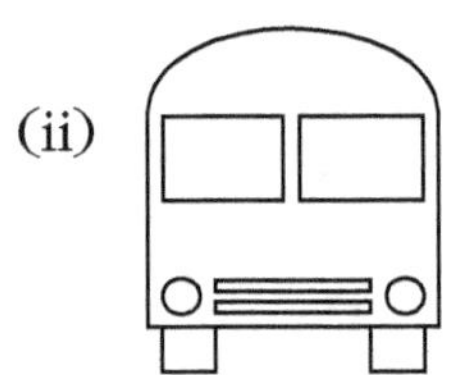

Standing lines   = __________

Sleeping lines   = __________

Curved lines   = __________

(iii) 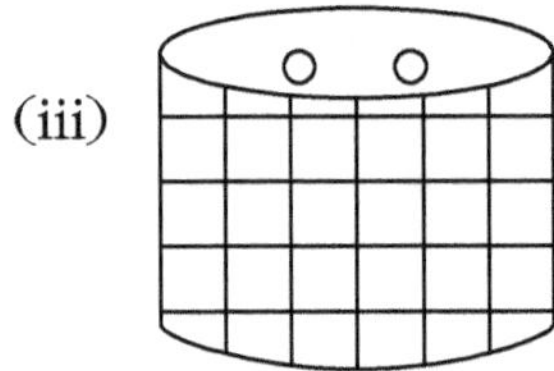

Standing lines   = __________

Sleeping lines   = __________

Curved lines   = __________

(iv) 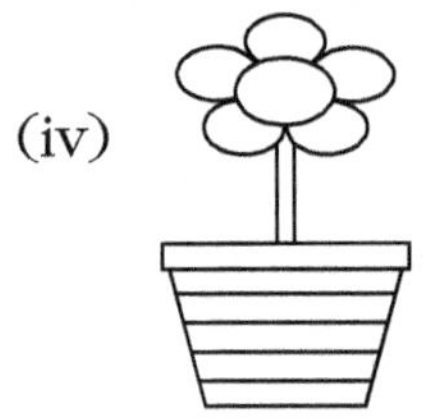

Standing lines   = __________

Sleeping lines   = __________

Curved lines   = __________

Give and Take

1 Find the sum. One has been done for you.

(i)
T	O
2	2
+	7
2	9

(ii)
T	O
4	2
+	5

(iii)
T	O
3	2
+	6

(iv)
T	O
2	5
+	2

(v)
T	O
1	1
+	8

(vi)
T	O
4	0
+	1

2 Find the sum. One has been done for you.

(i)
T	O
1	4
+ 1	7
3	1

(ii)
T	O
2	2
+ 1	9

(iii)
T	O
1	6
+ 2	5

(iv)
T	O
2	5
+ 1	7

(v)
T	O
1	9
+ 1	9

(vi)
T	O
3	4
+ 1	6

3 **Find the difference. One has been done for you.**

(i)

T	O
2	4
− 1	2
1	2

(ii)

T	O
4	3
− 2	3

(iii)

T	O
5	9
−	7

(iv)

T	O
3	8
− 1	7

(v)

T	O
3	9
− 2	9

(vi)

T	O
4	8
− 3	0

4 **Word problems.**

(i) 42 birds live in a garden. In winter, 38 birds also come in the garden. How many birds are there in the garden in winter?

(ii) On her friend's birthday, Yashu blew up 26 balloons. Meenal blew up 57. How many balloons did they blew together?

(iii) Vani made 30 paper boats. 10 boats sank. How many boats were left?

(iv) A man has to pack 63 toy cars and 12 dolls. He needs a box for each. How many boxes does he need?

(v) A large box of crayons has 55 crayons. A smaller box has 18 crayons less. How many crayons does the smaller box have?

(vi) Amy's mother is 50 yr old. Amy is 29 yr younger than his mother. How old is Amy now?

(vii) Roma has 14 dresses. Her mother gifted her 12 dresses more. How many dresses does Roma have now?

(viii) Sneha bought 73 bananas. Her brother ate 27 of them. How many bananas are left now?

5 Use the menu given below to find the total bill for each order.

Banana shake	₹ 20
Ice-cream	₹ 15
Burger large	₹ 30
Burger small	₹ 25
Orange juice	₹ 17
Lime soda	₹ 22

(i)

1 burger small =

1 lime soda =

+

Bill =

(ii)

1 banana shake =

1 ice-cream =

+

Bill =

(iii)

1 lime soda =

1 burger large =

+

Bill =

(iv)

1 orange juice = ⬜

1 burger small = ⬜

+

Bill = ⬜

6 Word problems on money.

(i) Annie gives ₹ 23 to Diana. If Annie had ₹ 66, how much money was she left with?

(ii) After buying some candies for ₹ 15, Alice had ₹ 28 left. How much money she had at the beginning?

(iii) Reena went to an amusement park with her mother. The cost of one adult ticket is ₹ 27 and the cost of one child ticket is ₹ 15. What is the total cost of both the tickets?

(iv) Aamya bought a winter cap for ₹ 33. She gave a ₹ 100 note to the shopkeeper. How much change did she receive?

(v) Rinkle sold his hockeystick for ₹ 35. He also sold the ball for ₹ 28. How much money does Rinkle have now?

(vi) Rony's father gave him ₹ 65 for lunch. He ate noodles for ₹ 18. How much money should he give back to his father?

The Longest Step

1 Tick (✓) the one having longest footstep in each part.

2 Study the picture carefully and use fingers given to answer the following questions.

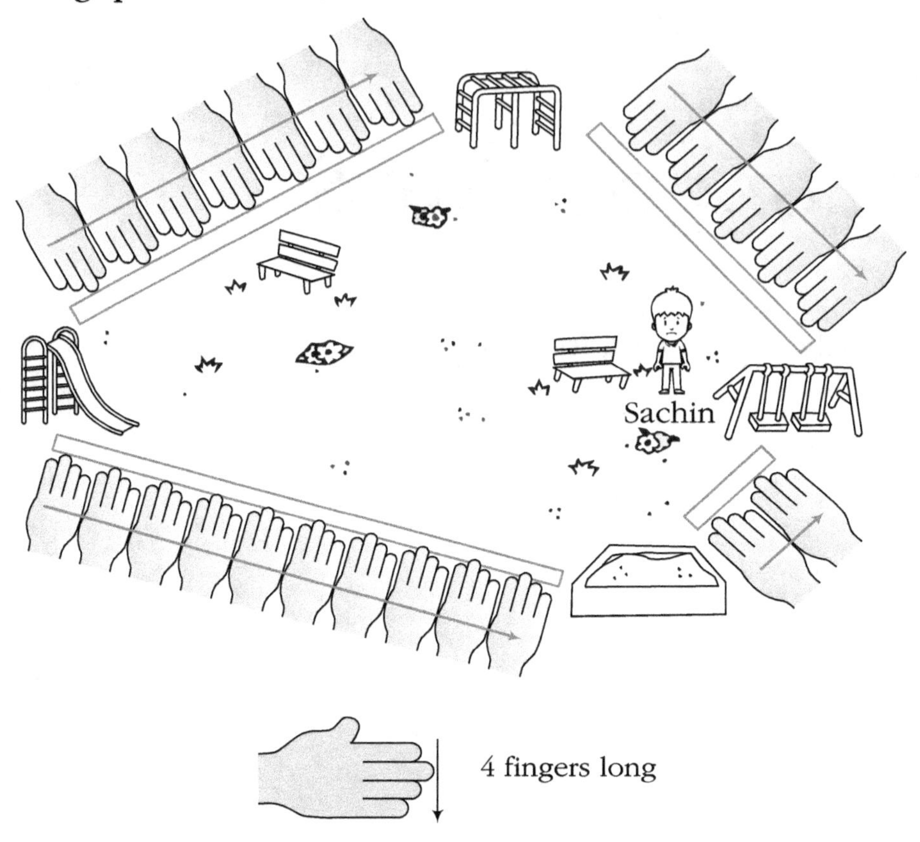

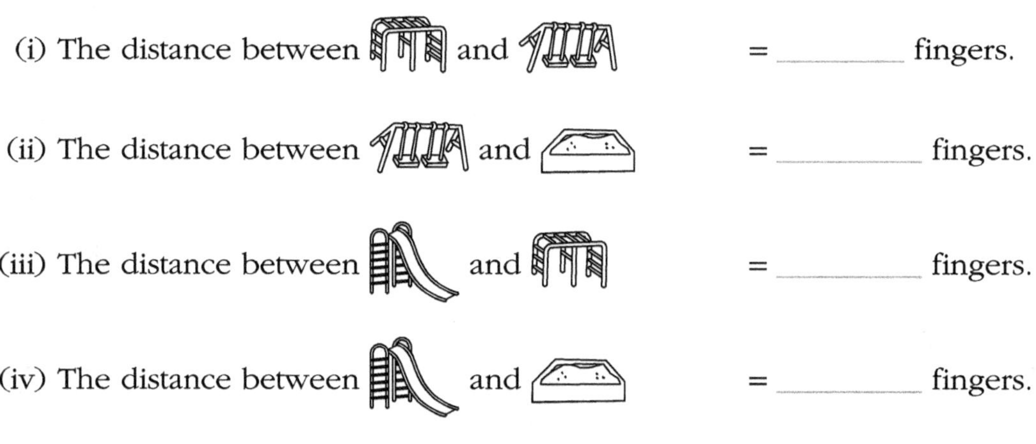

(i) The distance between 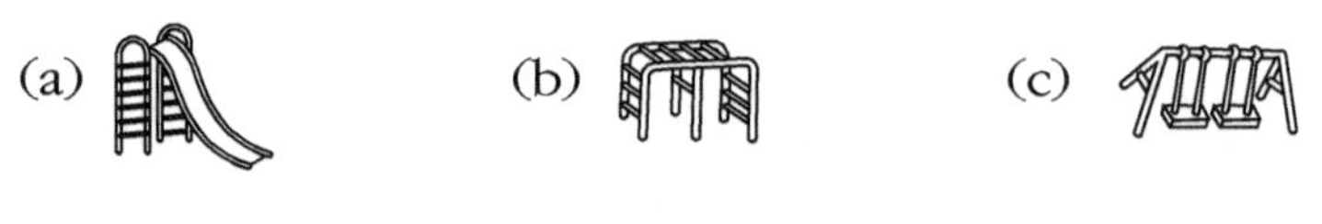 and = __________ fingers.

(ii) The distance between and = __________ fingers.

(iii) The distance between and = __________ fingers.

(iv) The distance between and = __________ fingers.

(v) Tick (✓) which is closest to Sachin.

(a)   (b)   (c)

3 Use the matchsticks shown below to measure the given objects.

(i) 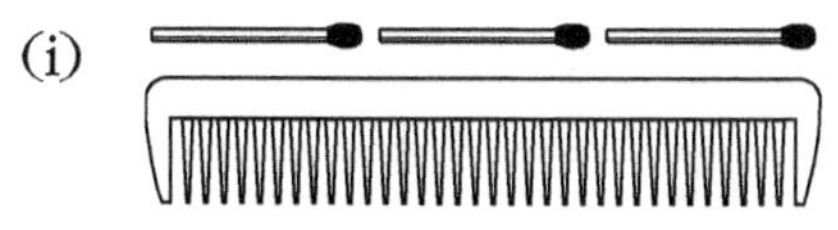

     matchsticks long

(ii) 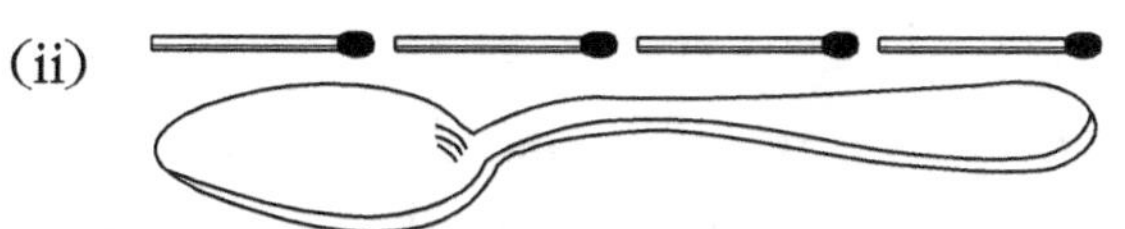

     matchsticks long

(iii) 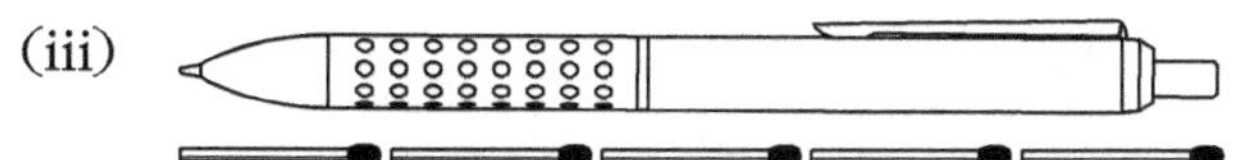

     matchsticks long

(iv) 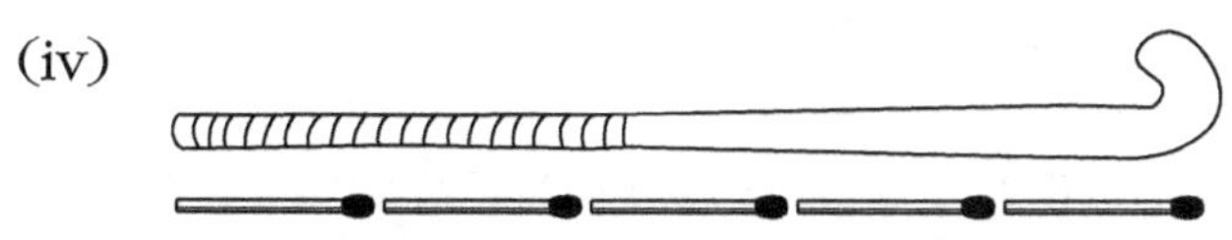

     matchsticks long

(v) 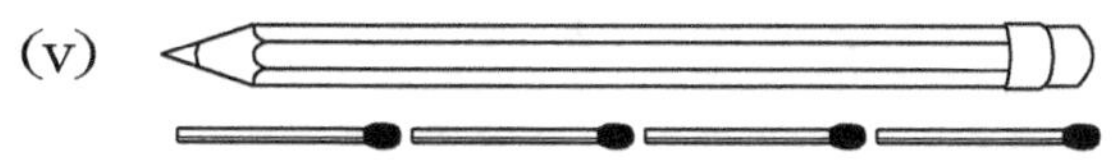

     matchsticks long

4 Find the length of the following objects using your arm length.

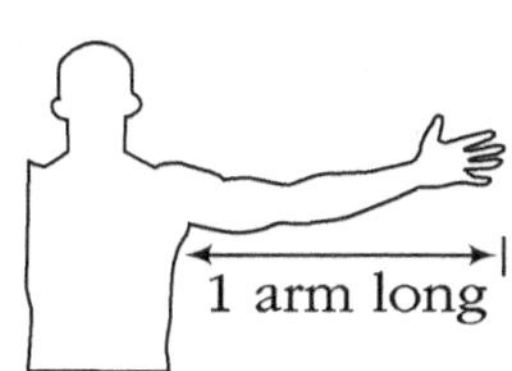

(i) 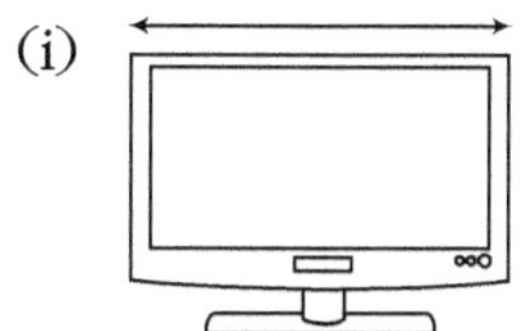

Your TV   = _____________ arm long

(ii) 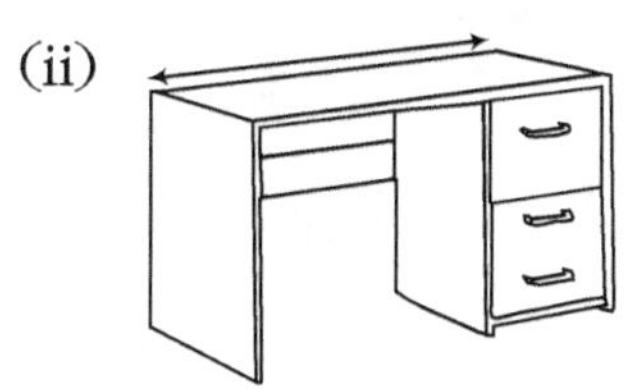

Your study table   = _____________ arm long

5 **Answer the following questions.**

(i) Name some units of measurement.

(a) _________________________   (b) _________________________

(c) _________________________   (d) _________________________

(ii) Mrinal measures the length of book as 3 handspans while Sebi measures it as 4 handspans and Kary measures it as 2 handspans. Whose handspan is longest among them?

(iii) Ruchi measures the length of a bat as 28 fingers, whereas Sam and Joy measure it as 24 fingers and 25 fingers, respectively. Whose finger is shortest?

Birds Come, Birds Go

1 Add the numbers. One has been done for you.

(i)
```
    2   5
  +     6
  ________
    3   1
```

(ii)
```
    4   8
  +     3
  ________
```

(iii)
```
    3   4
  +     8
  ________
```

(iv)
```
    1   9
  + 5   2
  ________
```

(v)
```
    7   5
  + 1   6
  ________
```

(vi)
```
    4   3
  + 3   7
  ________
```

(vii)
```
    6   5
  + 2   5
  ________
```

(viii)
```
    9   2
  +     7
  ________
```

(ix)
```
    3   3
  + 6   5
  ________
```

2 Subtract the numbers. One has been done for you.

(i)
```
    2   4
  –     9
  ───────
    1   5
  ───────
```

(ii)
```
    5   2
  – 1   8
  ───────
  ───────
```

(iii)
```
    3   8
  – 2   3
  ───────
  ───────
```

(iv)
```
    5   1
  – 4   3
  ───────
  ───────
```

(v)
```
    8   0
  – 2   8
  ───────
  ───────
```

(vi)
```
    6   5
  – 2   5
  ───────
  ───────
```

3 Word problems.

(i) A garden has 39 green birds and 42 red birds. How many total birds are there in the garden?

(ii) At a school carnival, a group of boys bought 47 tickets and a group of girls bought 46 tickets. How many tickets were bought in all?

(iii) There are 47 butterflies in the park out of which 19 flew away. How many butterflies are left in the park?

(iv) Anuj had 82 sweets. He gave 26 sweets to his sister. How many sweets are left with him?

(v) There are 20 frogs and 18 ducks in a pond. How many altogether in the pond?

(vi) Sumit scored 21 runs in a cricket match and Arun scored 33 runs. How many runs did they make in all?

(vii) Eagle A can eat 45 snakes in one month. Eagle B can eat 60 snakes in one month. Who can eat more snakes in a month and by how much?

4 **Solve the given sum and cross out the number in the table.**

53	24	31
59	16	70
65	42	78

(i) 43 + 27 = __________

(ii) 32 − 16 = __________

(iii) 76 − __________ = 23

(iv) 95 − 64 = __________

(v) 32 less than 91 = __________

(vi) 49 more than 29 = __________

(vii) The numbers left = __________

(viii) In the left numbers, the smallest number = __________

5 A group of children lives in a society having different building numbers. Find their building numbers by solving the questions written on cards. One has been done for you.

6 Children of clean toli counted the number of birds in the park.

Bird	Number of birds		Bird	Number of birds
Parrot	75		Cuckoo	95
Pigeon	89		Sparrow	64
Peacock	93			

(i) _______ birds were more than _______ birds. How many more?

____

____

(ii) Write the name of the bird which is least in number.

____

____

(iii) Write the name of the bird which is most in number.

____

____

(iv) Children counted more birds and got a total of 500. How many more birds did they count?

____

7 Find the sum on the flowers of Column I and match them with the pot having the same difference in Column II.

Column I		**Column II**

(i) 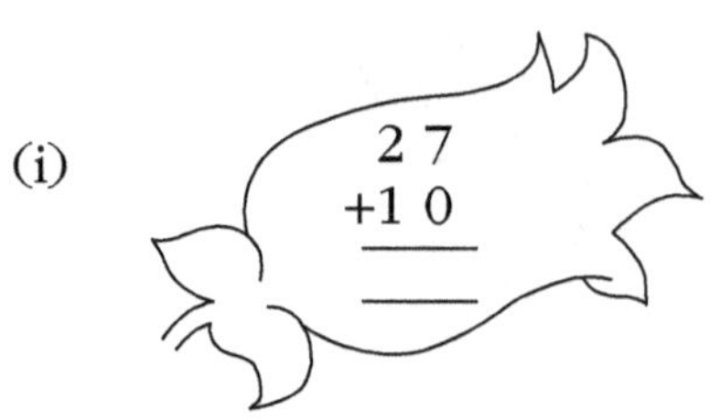

(a) 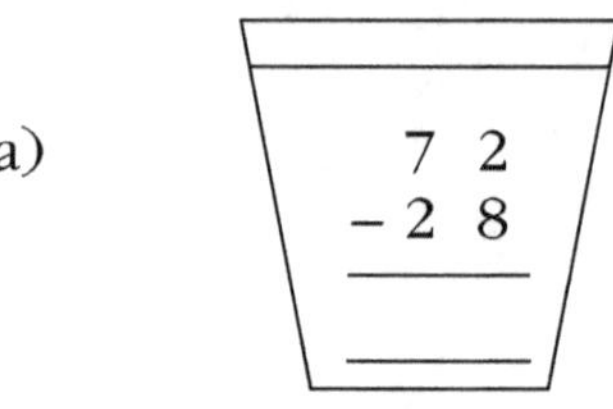

(ii) 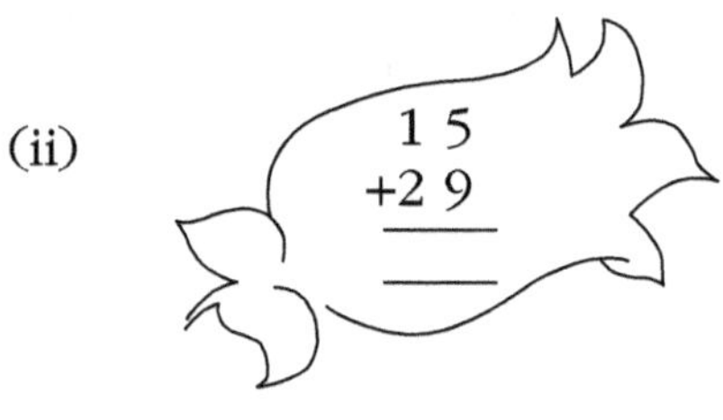

(b) 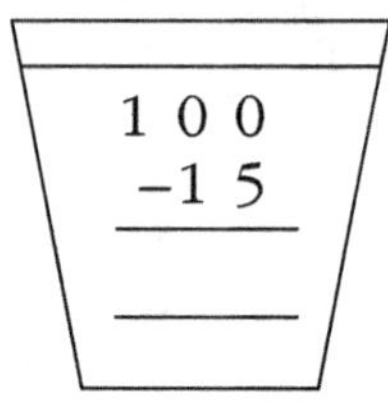

(iii) 

(c) 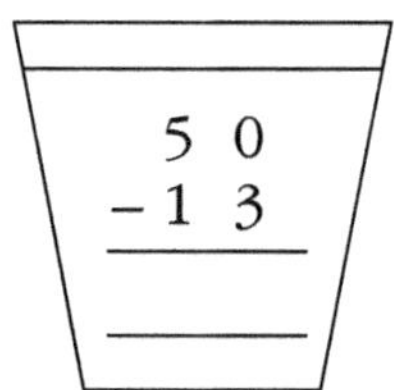

(iv) 

(d) 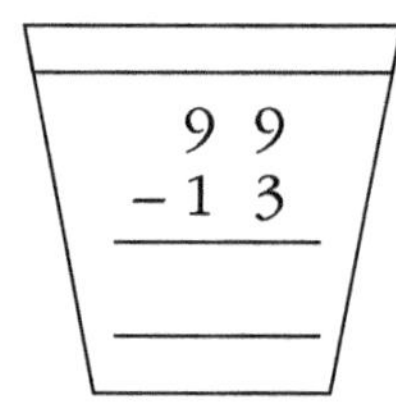

(v) 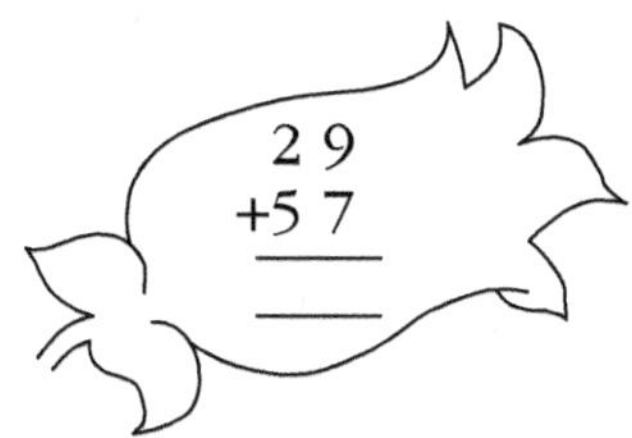

(e)

8 Money Problems

(i) Kiran collected ₹ 85 as fine from the class. She bought a duster and a chalk box for ₹ 20. She also bought 5 coloured chart papers for ₹ 25.

(a) The total money spent = ___________

(b) Money left with Kiran = ___________

(ii) James spent ₹ 24. Anoy spent ₹ 13 more than James.

(a) Money spent by Anoy = ___________

(b) Total money spent by both of them = ___________

(iii) Ajita bought two gifts for her friend for ₹ 34 and ₹ 26. She gave a ₹ 100 note to the shopkeeper.

(a) Total money spent on gifts = ___________

(b) Change received = ___________

9 Complete the multiplication fact for the following groups. One has been done for you.

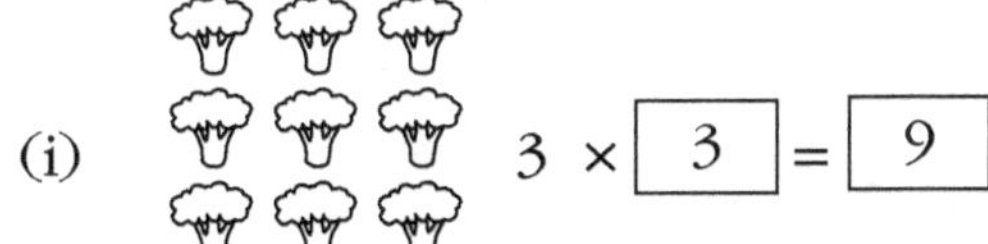

(i) $3 \times \boxed{3} = \boxed{9}$

(ii) $4 \times \boxed{} = \boxed{}$

(iii) $3 \times \boxed{} = \boxed{}$

(iv) $2 \times \boxed{} = \boxed{}$

(v) $4 \times \boxed{} = \boxed{}$

(vi) $4 \times \boxed{} = \boxed{}$

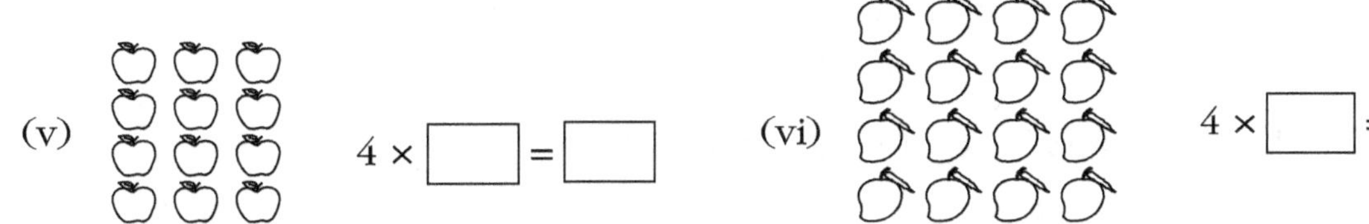

10 Rishi bought some stationery items from the shop.

Item	Cost (in ₹)
Pencil	4
Ruler	3
Book	40
Crayons	15
Eraser	5

Now, use the above list to answer the following questions.

(i) What is the difference between the cost of a Book and a pack of Crayons?

(ii) What is the total cost of a Pencil and pack of Crayons?

(iii) What is the total cost of all the items?

(iv) If Rishi gave a ₹ 100 note to the shopkeeper, for buying all items, then how much change will he get back?

Chapter 15

How Many Ponytails?

1 Four children made a table of their heights as shown below.

Name	Height
Tim	Shortest
Kary	Second tallest
Kate	Tallest
Tina	Third tallest

Using the above table, write down the names of the four children on the boards.

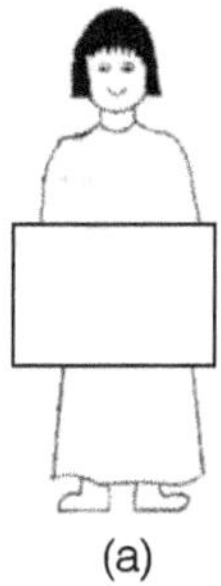

(a)

(b)

(c)

(d)

2 Sonam is making fruit juice for herself. She requires the following fruits for her juice.

Now, count the number of fruits and write it below.

	Fruit	Number of fruits
(i)	🍎	
(ii)	🍌	
(iii)	🍊	
(iv)		

3 In a birthday party, a group of girls came with different hair styles.

(i) Count the different hair styles and write the number below.

	Hair style	Number of girls		Hair style	Number of girls
(a)			(b)		
(c)			(d)		
(e)			(f)		

(ii) Tick (✓) on the most common hair style.

(a)   (b)   (c)

(iii) Tick (✓) on the least common hair style.

(a)   (b)   (c)

4 Jack has a bag which has some marbles hidden in it.

Make a list of the marbles in Jack's bag.

	Marble	Number of marbles
(i)	⦾	
(ii)	⊘	
(iii)	●	
(iv)	○	

Use the above list to answer the following questions.

(a) How many marbles more ○ than ⊘ does Jack have?

(b) How many marbles does Jack have in his bag?

____

(c) How many marbles less ○ than ⊙ does Jack have?

____

5 **Shinny makes a weather chart for July as shown below.**

Sun	Mon	Tue	Wed	Thu	Fri	Sat
	1 (Windy)	2 (Sunny)	3 (Cloudy)	4 (Cloudy)	5 (Windy)	6 (Rainy)
7 (Rainy)	8 (Windy)	9 (Cloudy)	10 (Sunny)	11 (Sunny)	12 (Cloudy)	13 (Cloudy)
14 (Cloudy)	15 (Cloudy)	16 (Rainy)	17 (Rainy)	18 (Rainy)	19 (Windy)	20 (Windy)
21 (Cloudy)	22 (Windy)	23 (Cloudy)	24 (Rainy)	25 (Cloudy)	26 (Cloudy)	27 (Sunny)
28 (Windy)	29 (Sunny)	30 (Sunny)	31 (Sunny)			

Key
Sunny
Windy
Cloudy
Rainy

Use the above information to answer the given questions.

	Key	Number of days
(i)	(Windy)	_____________
(ii)	(Sunny)	_____________
(iii)	(Cloudy)	_____________
(iv)	(Rainy)	_____________

(a) How many more days were sunny than rainy?

____

(b) How many more days were cloudy than windy?

____

Answers

Chapter 1 What is Long, What is Round?

1. (i) Round (ii) Long (iii) Round
   (iv) Long (v) Long (vi) Round
   (vii) Round (viii) Long

2. (i) Roll (ii) Roll (iii) Slide (iv) Slide (v) Roll (vi) Slide
   (vii) Roll (viii) Roll (ix) Roll (x) Slide (xi) Roll
   (xii) Side

5. (i), (iv)

6. (ii), (iii) and (v) can form a tower.

7. (i) long, round (ii) corner, flat
   (iii) roll, slide (iv) slide, roll

8. (i)-(d), (ii)-(a), (iii)-(b), (iv)-(c)

9. (i)-(a) (ii)-(a) (iii)-(a) (iv)-(b)

Chapter 2 Counting in Groups

1. (i) 12 (ii) 16 (iii) 18 (iv) 12

2. (ii) (a) 6 (b) $6 \times 3 = 18$
   (iii) (a) 5 (b) $5 \times 5 = 25$
   (iv) (a) 5 (b) $5 \times 4 = 20$

3. (i) (b) (ii) (b) (iii) (a)
   (iv) (b) (v) (a)

5. (i) 25, 27, 28, 29, 30, 31 (ii) 15, 16, 18, 19
   (iii) 38, 40, 41, 42 (iv) 40, 41, 42, 44, 45

6. (i) 17, 18, 19, 20, 21, 22, 23
   (ii) 57, 58, 59, 61, 62, 63, 64
   (iii) 33, 35, 36, 37, 38, 40
   (iv) 89, 90, 91, 92, 93, 94, 95

   (v) 46, 48, 49, 50, 51, 52
   (vi) 40, 41, 42, 43, 44, 45, 47
   (vii) 70, 71, 73, 74, 76, 77

7. (i) (a) Lewis (b) John
   (c) Odion (d) fifth
   (e) eighth
   (ii) 3 (iii) 9 (iv) 7

8. (i) fourth (ii) third
   (iii) fifth (iv) second

9. (ii) G-V (iii) F-VIII (iv) B-VI (v) C-II
   (vi) H-IV (vii) A-III (viii) E-VII

Chapter 3 How Much Can You Carry?

1. (i) (b) (ii) (a) (iii) (a) (iv) (b)

2. (i) (b) (ii) (b) (iii) (a) (iv) (a)

3. (i) Car (✓) (ii) Banana (✓)
   Jar (✗) Apple (✗)
   (iii) Woods (✓) (iv) Raj (✓)
   Container (✗) Rohan (✗)

4. (i) heavier (ii) lighter
   (iii) equal

5. (ii) (a) → A; (b) → B (iii) (a) → B; (b) → A
   (iv) (a) → A; (b) → B

6. (i), (iv)

7. (i) (b) (ii) (c) (iii) (a)

8. (ii) 6 (iii) 9 (iv) 6

9. (ii) (iii) (iv)

Chapter 4 Counting in Tens

1. (i) 8 (ii) $8 \times 10 = 80$ (iii) 7 (iv) 80, 87

2. (i) $5 \times 10 = 50$ (ii) $7 \times 10 = 70$
   (iii) $9 \times 10 = 90$ (iv) 4

3. (i) 5 (ii) 10 (iii) 5 (iv) 55
   (v) $4 \times 10 = 40$

4. (ii) $\boxed{5\,|\,2}$, $\boxed{52}$ (iii) $\boxed{7\,|\,6}$, $\boxed{76}$

5. (i) (a)   (ii) (a)

Chapter 5 Patterns

2. (i) 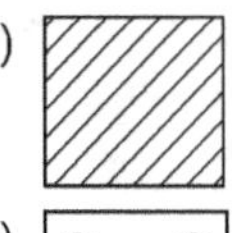   (ii)

(iii)   (iv)

(v)   (vi)

(ii) ▽△▽△▽

(iii) 🍎🍎🍎🍎🍎

(iv) △☆⇧△☆

(v)

3. (i) (a)   (ii) (b)   (iii) (c)   (iv) (c)

4. (c)

5. (i) ♡◇♡◇♡

6. (i) 10, 12, 14, 16   (ii) 29, 30, 31, 32
(iii) 45, 48, 51, 54   (iv) 68, 78, 88, 98
(v) 30, 35, 40, 45

7. (i) DD, EE, FF   (ii) dd, ee, ff
(iii) G, I, K   (iv) 44, 55, 66
(v) 40, 50, 60

8. 24, 32, 40, 48, 56

Chapter 6 Footprints

1. (i)-(b)   (ii)-(d)   (iii)-(a)   (iv)-(c)

2. (ii)-(c)   (iii)-(e)   (iv)-(a)   (v)-(f)
(vi)-(d)

4. Do yourself

5. (i) 12   (ii) 13   (iii) 9   (iv) 13

Chapter 7 Jugs and Mugs

1. 5

2. (ii) 3 lemons   (iii) 5 lemons
(iv) 7 lemons

3. (i) ₹ 40   (ii) ₹ 80   (iii) ₹ 60   (iv) (a)

4. (i) Dropper   (ii) Bucket   (iii) Cup
(iv) Dropper, Cup, Bottle, Jug, Bucket

5. (i) 1 glass   (ii) 24

6. (i) 4   (ii) 16   (iii) 9   (iv) 18

Chapter 8 Tens and Ones

1.
(ii) ₹ 10 → 9   ₹ 1 → 5   (iii) ₹ 10 → 6   ₹ 1 → 7

(iv) ₹ 10 → 2   ₹ 1 → 8   (v) ₹ 10 → 3   ₹ 1 → 7

(vi) ₹ 10 → 1   ₹ 1 → 2

2. (ii) (a) ₹ 10 + ₹ 10 + ₹ 10 + ₹ 10 + ₹ 1 + ₹ 1
+ ₹ 1 + ₹ 1
(b) Four ₹ 10 notes and four ₹ 1 coins

(iii) (a) ₹ 10 + ₹ 1 + ₹ 1 + ₹ 1 + ₹ 1 + ₹ 1 + ₹ 1 + ₹ 1
(b) One ₹ 10 note and seven ₹ 1 coins

(iv) (a) ₹ 10 + ₹ 10 + ₹ 10 + ₹ 1 + ₹ 1 + ₹ 1
+ ₹ 1 + ₹ 1
(b) Three ₹ 10 notes and five ₹ 1 coins

3. (ii) ₹ 26   (iii) ₹ 46   (iv) ₹ 52   (v) ₹ 27

4. (ii) 90, 7   (iii) 60   (iv) 29   (v) 80, 3
   (vi) 2   (vii) 50, 8   (viii) 20   (ix) 60, 9
   (x) 80, 2

5. (i) (a) ₹ 13   (b) ₹ 16   (c) ₹ 15
   (d) ₹ 16   (e) ₹ 19
   (ii) Sujata   (iii) Rekha

(iv) Meera and Karan

6. (ii) 20, 3   (iii) 10, 8   (iv) 20, 6

8. (ii) 4, 8   (iii) 6, 3   (iv) 7, 5   (v) 8, 7

9. (i) 7, 8   (ii) 6, 5   (iii) 5, 9   (iv) 8, 3
   (v) 2

Chapter 9 My Funday

1. (i) (c)   (ii) (a)   (iii) (b)   (iv) (d)

2. (i) Tuesday   (ii) Saturday
   (iii) Tuesday   (iv) Thursday
   (v) Saturday   (vi) Thursday

3. I. (ii) Monday, Saturday
   (iii) Monday, Saturday
   (iv) Monday, Tuesday, Wednesday, Thursday, Friday
   (v) Monday, Tuesday, Wednesday, Thursday
   (vi) Tuesday, Wednesday, Friday
   (vii) Tuesday, Thursday, Saturday
   (viii) Wednesday, Thursday
   (ix) Wednesday, Friday

II. (i) 2   (ii) Friday, Saturday
   (iii) Saturday

4. (i) Monday, Thursday   (ii) Saturday
   (iii) Computer, Hindi   (iv) Saturday
   (v) Maths, English

6. B. (iv)-(b)   C. (i)-(e)
   D. (v)-(d)   E. (ii)-(c)

7. (i) False   (ii) True   (iii) True
   (iv) False   (v) True   (vi) False

8. (i) January   (ii) June   (iii) December
   (iv) September
   (v) July, August
   (vi) (a) (✔) (b) (✗) (c) (✗) (d) (✔)

Chapter 10 Add Our Points

1. (i) 25   (ii) 39   (iii) 16   (iv) 9
   (v) (a) 58 (b) 51

2. (i) 20   (ii) 19   (iii) 24   (iv) 21
   (v) 11   (vi) 6   (vii) 40   (viii) 31

3. (i) (c)   (ii) (c)   (iii) (b)

4. (i) 2   (ii) 5
   (iii) 5   (iv) 5   (v) 4

5. (ii) One ₹ 10 note and one ₹ 20 note
   (iii) One ₹ 2 coin and one ₹ 1 coin

(iv) One ₹ 10 note and one ₹ 5 coin

6. (i) 41   (ii) 35   (iii) 33
   (iv) 32   (v) 54

7. (ii) 23   (iii) 15   (iv) 24
   (v) 14   (vi) 21   (vii) 16

8. (i) 3 + 4 = 7   (ii) 7 + 4 = 11
   (iii) 8 + 11 = 19

9. (i) Reena   (ii) Jyoti   (iii) 66 times
   (iv) Priya

10. (ii) 10 kg   (iii) 17 kg   (iv) 18 kg

Chapter 11 Lines and Lines

1. (i) Sleeping   (ii) Standing
   (iii) Slanting   (iv) Slanting
   (v) Curved   (vi) Slanting

2. (i)-(d)   (ii)-(a)
   (iii)-(b)   (iv)-(c)

3. (i) (✔)   (ii) (✗)
   (iii) (✔)   (iv) (✗)
   (v) (✔)   (vi) (✔)

4. (i) (a)-4 (b)-5
   (ii) (a)-5 (b)-4
   (iii) (a)-6 (b)-9

5. Straight lines-3

Curved lines-2

7. (i) 7

(ii) 9

(iii) 2

Chapter **12** Give and Take

1. (ii) 47 (iii) 38 (iv) 27 (v) 19
(vi) 41

2. (ii) 41 (iii) 41 (iv) 42 (v) 38
(vi) 50

3. (ii) 20 (iii) 52 (iv) 21 (v) 10
(vi) 18

Chapter **13** The Longest Step

1. (i) (c) (ii) (b) (iii) (c)

2. (i) 20 (ii) 8 (iii) 28
(iv) 40 (v) (c)

Chapter **14** Birds Come, Birds Go

1. (ii) 51 (iii) 42 (iv) 71 (v) 91
(vi) 80 (vii) 90 (viii) 99 (ix) 98

2. (ii) 34 (iii) 15
(iv) 8 (v) 52
(vi) 40

3. (i) 81 (ii) 93 (iii) 28 (iv) 56
(v) 38 (vi) 54 (vii) Eagle B, 15

(i) ₹ 25 (ii) ₹ 19 (iii) ₹ 67 (iv) ₹ 33

4. (i) 70 (ii) 16 (iii) 53 (iv) 31
(v) 59 (vi) 78 (vii) 24, 65, 42

Chapter **15** How Many Ponytails?

1. (a) Kate (b) Kary
(c) Tina (d) Tim

2. (i) 5 (ii) 3 (iii) 6 (iv) 2

3. (i) (a) 1 (b) 3 (c) 3 (d) 3
(e) 3 (f) 4
(ii) (a) (iii) (b)

8.

	Standing lines	Sleeping lines	Curved lines
(i)	4	5	3
(ii)	14	11	3
(iii)	7	4	4
(iv)	4	7	6

4. (i) 80 (ii) 83 (iii) 20 (iv) 75
(v) 37 (vi) 21 yr (vii) 26 (viii) 46

5. (i) ₹ 47 (ii) ₹ 35 (iii) ₹ 52 (iv) ₹ 42

6. (i) ₹ 43 (ii) ₹ 43 (iii) ₹ 42 (iv) ₹ 67
(v) ₹ 63 (vi) ₹ 47

3. (i) 3 (ii) 4 (iii) 5
(iv) 5 (v) 4

5. (ii) Kary (iii) Ruchi

(viii) 24

5. (ii) 73 (iii) 59 (iv) 73
(v) 56 (vi) 73 (vii) 56
(vii) 59 (ix) 59

6. (i) 11 (ii) Sparrow
(iii) Cuckoo (iv) 84

7. (i) – (c) (ii) – (a) (iii) – (e)
(iv) – (b) (v) – (d)

8. (i) (a) 45 (b) 40 (ii) (a) 37 (b) 61
(iii) (a) 60 (b) 40

9. (ii) 8 (iii) 15 (iv) 10
(v) 12 (vi) 196

4. (i) 5 (ii) 4 (iii) 4 (iv) 6
(a) 2 (b) 19 (c) 1

5. (i) 7 (ii) 7 (iii) 11 (iv) 6
(a) 1 (b) 4

www.ingramcontent.com/pod-product-compliance
Lightning Source LLC
LaVergne TN
LVHW060601200726
843509LV00003B/177